MW01140442

Feeling Better: A Field Guide to Liking Yourself

Andrea Loewen

Published by Andrea Loewen, 2018.

FEELING BETTER: A FIELD GUIDE TO LIKING YOURSELF

First edition. October 27, 2018.

Copyright © 2018 Andrea Loewen.

ISBN: 978-1999506414

Written by Andrea Loewen.

Table of Contents

Introduction

My name is Andrea, and I used to hate myself.

I never thought about it quite such strong terms, but for the bulk of my teens and early twenties (well, let's be honest, as far back as I can remember) every decision I made, every thought, opinion, and feeling I had stemmed out of a deep-seeded belief that I was, basically, worthless. That I had nothing to offer, that nobody really liked me, and most definitely that nobody would ever really love me. These beliefs created the container for my experience of life, and I experienced a lot of loneliness, deep sadness, and depression.

These days, I like myself. I think I'm a good person, that I offer things to the world, am intelligent, and am both likeable and lovable. This shift has completely changed my life. It didn't change my job, my relationship status, or how good I was at sticking to an exercise regimen, but it did change the way I experienced every single moment of my life: my thoughts and feelings, which, of course, impacted my approach to my job, romantic life, and self-care practices on a fundamental level. I no longer experienced every single thing that happened in my life through a filter of self-loathing and worthlessness. Since the one constant I have in life is myself, this change in perspective altered everything.

So what happened? Did I have what Oprah would call an "ah-ha!" moment that changed everything? Yes, actually. As a relationship unravelled, something in my heart and head connected, and I said, "Ah-ha! I am worth something!" (More on that later.) But that wasn't enough. The hatred was pretty embedded at that point, and ınoment wasn't going to unravel it. I kept digging in. I saw counsellors and read more books. I did online quizzes, had faltering conversations with my mom and a small handful of trusted friends where I admitted little portions of what I was going through, and, at the end of the day, I tried out a lot of different things to see what would help me change the way I saw myself.

This book represents my experience of working through years of depression and, by extension, the deep self-hatred at the root of it. It is a collection of the things that worked for me: the practices, experiences, and realizations, humbly offered in the hopes that they might help you or someone you love who may be living in a period of darkness, feeling stuck, unlovable, and hopeless, or who may be feeling crushed by the weight of a depression.

Sharing it is pretty much the scariest thing I've ever done.

A Brief History of My Self-Hatred

It's hard to pin down exactly where my self-hatred came from. There is no lightbulb memory of being told I was stupid or someone yelling, "I hate you!" back at me. Instead, I just remember being quite certain from a very young age that everyone who was friends with me was only fulfilling some sense of pity or obligation, that they really could barely tolerate my presence and were happier when I wasn't there. I remember playing with my siblings and cousins with a constant low-grade expectation that one day they were going to turn around and say, "We can't take it anymore, we hate you, and you have to leave." And then I would be alone forever.

The only things that gave me any sense of worth were my accomplishments, so I worked hard, got good grades, and joined clubs. I kept busy to avoid putting my heart on the line or facing the terrible voices inside that said, "No one will ever love you, and nobody does. You are mediocre at best, annoying to be around, and horribly undesirable." It sounds ridiculous and over the top, but when we stop and pay attention, the dark voices in our minds usually are just that—ridiculous and over the top. I foresaw a life where everyone would grow tired of pretending they liked me, leaving me all alone to wither away in a prolonged epilogue with no one who even cared to witness it.

It may not be a surprise, in light of this, that I spent the majority of my high school and university years dealing with depression that varied in severity, although very few people knew about it. It was hugely important for me to maintain a pleasant façade, and it turns out that you can be depressed and still have an innate personality that is pretty upbeat. When you are known as "the happy one" people are willing to accept almost any explanation as to why you seem down, or "not yourself", at the moment.

But one day, during my first year at university, the façade broke. I began weeping in front of my mom over a completely minor problem: I couldn't get a ride to see a friend. It was obvious to her (and my sister who happened to be in the car) that there was something else going on. Everything came pouring out, and with her help, I began seeing a counsellor. Since then, I've done all the thing we do to help ourselves: counselling, pastoral care, reading all the books, and studying psychology. From these, I put together a few tools and concepts that created the foundation for my healing. It didn't happen all at once; healing came in many, many phases.

The first and clearest phase of healing (also known as my "ah-ha!" moment) arrived because of a boy. (Yes, I do have a strong dose of feminist annoyance that my self-love realization came at the hands of a boy and not myself or a posse of powerful women, but what can you do? Facts are facts.)

I didn't have my first boyfriend until I was 23 years old, the age that, as a teenager, I had assumed would see me blissfully married. (Looking back, it's a bit funny that the girl who thought everyone hated her also expected to find a husband by 23 years old, but we are nothing if not a mess of contradictions.) I was behind schedule, and not particularly happy about it, when I met him. We were terrible for each other, but by the time we realized it we were too in love to be realistic, and it was the existence of this boyfriend and, perhaps surprisingly, our break-up, that helped me locate my first inkling that I was deserving of love. It didn't even occur to me as a possibility before then. Not, that is, until we were having a fight. He told me I was being too negative about myself, a statement I found hilarious because he was negative about *everything*. He then countered that he was negative about other people—but that he, in fact, thought he was pretty awesome.

My brain stopped for a moment and I almost laughed out loud. He thought *he* was awesome? And I, who was empirically much more awesome than him, thought I was worthless? A brief moment of clarity! At that moment, I realized two things. First, I saw a glimpse of how doomed our relationship was: if your significant other calls themselves awesome and you want to roll your eyes and laugh at them, that's a bad sign. Secondly, and importantly, this marked the first time I was able to truly see my dark voices for what they really were: terrible lies. I was suddenly aware that somewhere inside of me, I believed I had value.

So it was this boyfriend who, unbeknownst to him, showed me that I was worthy of at least one person's love, gave me one surreal moment of clarity about my own worth, and when we finally broke up, let me see that I was strong enough to walk away when it wasn't working. Sure, it took me months of knowing we were bad news to actually have the guts to do something about it, but it was a step, and it surprised me. It made me look at myself more closely because I couldn't think of any other time I had walked away from external validation by my own free will. I must have been stronger than I realized if I had been able to do that, right?

Still, those old lies can still be a struggle for me. My core beliefs may have changed, but I spent twenty-five years telling myself that I was basically comprised of badness. This kind of reinforcement takes more undoing than one simple revelation.

To greatly simplify cognitive psychology and neuroscience, our thoughts create pathways in our brains. The more you think something, the more efficient and well worn that path gets. The pathways in my brain became very, very efficient in transmitting terrible thoughts of self-loathing and undeservedness. Some shades of those thoughts are still present. But now, at the very least, I know that they are lies, and I have some tools to combat them. Tools that I am excited to share with you!

How to Use This Book

My hope for this book is that sharing my experiences and the tools that worked for me might inspire and help those of you who may be struggling to recognize and value your own self-worth. One of the most difficult aspects of depression is it blocks us from seeing ourselves as we should: as creatures worthy of the awe, love, dignity, and respect.

It's arranged by topic, so you don't have to read through from start to finish. If you're most interested in how spiritual practices might connect to self-worth, jump ahead to Chapter 13, but if you'd rather look into cognitive exercises, go to Chapter 3. To read about dealing with a dating life populated only with tumbleweeds, go to Chapter 9. Or if you'd like to read about small day-to-day choices you can make, like actually wearing the clothes you want to wear, that's here too, in Chapter 8.

Like everything else in your life, how you work with this book is your own choice. You can read it front to back or you can bounce around to different chapters as you see fit. You can try out my practices exactly as I did them, or alter them to suit you. You may wish to read this book in concert with other supports, including reading it alongside a trusted friend or loved one, a counsellor, mental health professional, or while on a new journey with medication.

Most of all, I hope that this book will offer some hope that change is possible, as well as some practical tools that might help bring that change to your life. Keeping in mind that healing is a multifaceted and individual journey, nothing in this book is intended to be taken all on its own, without adjustment or external support. Almost everything in it came from another source and then was adjusted to fit my own specific needs. I hope you will feel empowered to do the same and will gather any and all additional supports required.

Chapter 1- Because You Are a Creature of Awe

"I like you, just the way you are." - Mr. Rogers

You are awesome. If you can read that sentence and know in the deepest part of your heart that it's true, then you are probably already rocking the awesome life and can keep at it. If the sentence makes you recoil in terror, think, "Maybe...I guess," or respond with an over-compensatory, "Well, duh, I'm the best thing to ever exist in all of existence!" (thus hiding your secret feelings of self-loathing), then we should talk.

Before we go any further, I'll draw your attention to the word I'm going to use a lot: awesome. I know that word gets over-used these days. Almost everything on the internet is awesome, whether it's a kitten running head first into a wall or a picture of Ian McKellan in a funny t-shirt. (Okay, I'll be honest, I would like to have more pictures of Ian McKellan in funny t-shirts in my life.) (Also, kittens are adorable.)

Here is my definition of awesome, for the purposes of this book: that I am, as a human being, a creature of awe. That I am, as some might say, "fearfully and wonderfully made."

Now, before all the atheists start throwing their hackles in the air: I'm not saying you need to accept a Creator God here. The science of evolution is a truly wondrous origin story (read some Carl Sagan and let's talk), and no matter how we got here, it still points to something awe-inspiring inside all of us. We as humans are, without question, a whole that is greater than the sum of our parts, and that is *awesome*.

The beauty of this is that awesomeness is completely unearned. I am not awesome because I have done something awesome, because I look awesome, or because I have learned how to talk like those hip youngsters. I am awesome, first and foremost, because I am a person and that's *what people are*. So are you.

I didn't always see things this way. I used to perceive my value (if I had it at all) as based on my accomplishments, what I had produced. While there is some good that results from this worldview, like providing the drive to actually contribute something to society, I now see it as more dangerous than not. If my true value comes only from what I produce, I am under constant pressure to keep going, keep performing, keep creating, and do more, more, more. There is never the freedom to stop, lest everyone see what a failure of a human I really am underneath it all. Meanwhile, feelings of envy at those who somehow manage to achieve more than me (because there always will be, and they will have done it before they were 21!), and silent scorn for those who do not live up to my standard, cloud my mind.

That was no way for me to live, and I don't think it's a good way for anyone to live. Valuing life based on what it produces breeds score-keeping, comparison, jealousy, dehumanization, and a deep, abiding terror. Psychologist Albert Ellis divides the concept into those of love and acceptance in his book *In His Own Words*: "You love a person because he or she has lovable traits, but you accept everyone just because they're alive and human." To this, I'd like to add that you love a person not because of what they have accomplished or how well they stack up to all the other humans, but because of the person that they are. My parents are wonderful, regular people. I am proud of the things they accomplished in their lives and the good they have done, but I wouldn't love them more if they were superstars. On the flipside, there are people in this world I don't particularly like or agree with. I don't support the work that they do, nor do I want to spend much time with them. They are still fully human and beautiful creatures. I get angry sometimes and mourn what I see as the harm they do, but this does not diminish their acceptance into humanity and its inherent value.

A life based on accomplishments and comparison, intended to protect me, bred brokenness and deep self-loathing. But as I shifted towards a place where I could begin appreciating my own self-worth separate of impressive lists of accomplishments, I became more attuned to the wondrous existence of life, consciousness, imagination, and breath. Rather than brokenness and self-loathing, that new attunement truly bred awe.

I mean, come on! Look at us! Look at the overwhelming intricacy of how our bodies are assembled, at the beauty of relationships. Does the fact that we can form these invisible worlds with other people and see ourselves in one another not amaze you?

If you would like to read a novel that really illuminates the wondrousness of humanity read *The Humans* by Matt Haig. It is a comical take on what it means to be a human in the modern era, poking fun at our ridiculous foibles while marvelling at our glory.

So there's the universal awesomeness of humanity and existence. Then there is the unique awesomeness of who we are as individuals, and much of that greatness lies in the fact that we live in multitudes, that we are messy. So the first thing we have to do is not only acknowledge, but embrace that messy humanity. We all have a mixture of traits, habits, and passions that help and hinder us, drawing on beauty and ugliness, joy and pain, and if we don't start being honest with ourselves about them, we are missing out on the opportunity to experience true love for ourselves.

For example, I am taller than the average girl, but avoided a lifetime of hunching because of two things: my dad telling me that tall women are graceful when I was young enough to believe him and a lifetime of ballet and yoga. That said, I still feel like an ogre at times, and that will probably never change. I passionately love the arts, specifically theatre, literature, and dance, but I think Shakespeare is overrated as a playwright (although a spectacular poet). Since I was a child I wanted to have at least five careers, and I seem to be right on track for multi-tasking my way through life, which basically means I have a very hard time saying no to things and wind up doling out a lot of half-measures. I have a lot of friends and am super outgoing, but have few truly close relationships. In fact, recently I discovered that the people who aren't right in front of me get ignored more than I would like to admit. My first kiss happened at 19 and it was a deeply unsettling experience. The ballerina Karen Kain was my childhood hero, and now I fantasize about time travelling with Doctor Who. I love learning and sharing knowledge, which can make me an insufferable know-it-all sometimes. I want to somehow live a life that is simultaneously on-the-edge-of-the-grid rural and that of an urbane socialite and artist. I have always been a little bit of a hippie and a little bit of a punk. I spill on myself at least once a day and hope it's part of my charm. I'm funny, at least to me, everything makes me cry, and I often talk a little too loud.

This might sound like I am trying to be adorable in the sharing of my flaws, but let me be clear: I am not proud of the negative traits in that list. I get embarrassed every time someone points out I've been talking too loud and am working hard to have deeper, truly vulnerable relationships. Not only is it impossible to make any changes if you don't recognize your own faults (more on that in Chapter 12), but truly loving oneself requires embracing all parts of who you are.

This could easily lead to a lot of shame if I looked at the negative side without the balance of positives, without the compassion for humanity (where literally nobody is perfect), without a sense of humour, and without a belief that I have inherent value that is not impacted by these things.

What about you? What is your cocktail of beautiful-yet-conflicting traits, both positive and negative? Your sum that is greater than its parts? Because we all have it. We are all awesome, as individuals and as members of the universal beauty of human existence.

And yet, many of us walk around tearing our poor little hearts and souls to pieces at every turn, determining our worth based on what we can accomplish, or worse, the attention we get from others. We compare ourselves constantly, either to other people or our imagined, idealized selves. Never satisfied, never enough, never worthy. Hoping to cover up our terrible lack in any way possible, fearing that if anyone saw the real us, they would no longer even be able to pretend to love us.

I did this for a very long time. I know now not everyone else has the same story—as an adult, I was amazed when I found out that some of my friends have always liked and respected themselves, asking them with disbelief, "You mean you didn't hate yourself growing up?" However, I know that I am not the only one who has lived in this self-persecution.

You aren't alone. You also don't have to continue to live this way.

Making Awesomeness Work for You

I offer no promises of eternal happiness, disappearing problems, career satisfaction, thrilling romance, or skinny thighs. In fact, happiness is beside the point. I don't think life is about being happy—happiness is a feeling, and like all feelings, it comes and goes. Experiencing one feeling all the time doesn't seem particularly healthy given the ever-changing circumstances of life. What I am offering in this book is a toolkit for shifting our foundational beliefs about who we are and what we are worth, specifically, shifting them from a place of self-loathing to self-acceptance (and maybe even self-love!)

To be clear on this, I see one objective reality about each of us: the truth of our worthiness. This is an integral part of who we all are that will never change, no matter what else is happening. As we grow older and experience life we will change, maybe a lot, but interwoven through it all is the reality that we are all creatures of awe.

Once you have learned to see that you are worthy of awe, you will be able to go on to live your life meaningfully. You might even be able to make the subtle shift from feeling the need to prove your worth through constant productivity to using your worth tribute things of value in this world.

The difference is crucial to your own well-being: if you are producing to prove that you deserve to use up the oxygen you breathe, then it will never be enough and you will be a slave to the approval of others. If, on the other hand, you contribute out of a belief in your own worth, the act becomes more of an offering. Ego (while always present in those of us who aren't Jesus or Buddha) plays a much smaller role. You don't need to pump it all out right away, and you don't need the accolades of others. Or at the very least, you know that you aren't a waste if it doesn't go well. It's the difference between creation that is self-serving or self-sacrificing.

This means that there are two parts to all of this. The first is recognizing your worthiness, all on your own. That's the discovery of what's already there, a sort of archeological dig. The second is creating meaning out of that discovery. It's locating your particular awesomeness and deciding what you can do with it.

Leo C. Rosten said in his essay "The Myths by Which We Live" (in a quote often attributed to Ralph Waldo Emerson), "The purpose of life is not to be happy. It is to be useful, to be honourable, to be compassionate, to have it make some difference that you have lived and lived well." This notion of living well, of finding meaning over happiness, resonates nicely with me. It places the focus outside of ourselves and onto something bigger and better than us. On what we can give, not in a desperate attempt to add to a pile of "good" to outweigh the infinite "bad" on the other side, but simply to add. To give generously and freely, because we have something worth giving.

There's a hint at something else important in there: realizing your intrinsic worthiness does not mean thinking you are better or bigger than anyone or anything else. We are each a tiny part of existence, and we have influence over very little of it. But from a root of meaning and worthiness, we can create something meaningful.

I can't give you a revelation. I can't make you suddenly see your beautiful, meaningful, awe-inspiring self. I wish I could. I wish I could arrange life circumstances for you in such a way that you'll have a sudden moment of clarity.

Chances are, though, if you're reading this, you already know. Somewhere deep inside of you is the glimmer of knowledge that when you say that you are a worthless being, you are lying to yourself. Otherwise, why would you have even bothered to pick this book up?

Now I'm going to give you a very important warning: this book is not meant to replace anything else you might need, including counselling, medication, access to healthcare resources, or access to professionals like psychologists or psychiatrists—I am none of those things. I would like to point out that my experiences with depression have strong roots in my terrible false beliefs about my own self-worth. I am whole-heartedly supportive of people getting whatever they need to feel like themselves—for the short term, while they find the tools to manage things on their own, or for the long term, as they draw from a variety of resources that may include psychiatry, counselling, social services, medication, leave from work, a new professional path more aligned with one's mental health needs, support groups, and more. Everyone experiences depression differently. Everyone faces different monsters, and while my monsters might resemble yours, they are different. I learned how to fight my monsters, but I don't know what your monsters' secret powers are. Don't rob yourself of any necessary tools to fight them just because I don't mention them in this book.

Go Your Own Way

Everything I share with you in this book should be taken in and filtered through your own experiences. In my yoga teacher training I was given some advice to follow whenever learning from a guru, and while I wouldn't put myself in the guru's seat, I still think it applies:

> 1) Listen like a deer listens to music. (Translation: be attentive and listen closely to the true meaning of what's being given to you).

> 2) Digest it like a cow digests grass. (Translation: over and over again—really mull over the meaning of what's being given to you and how it might realistically fit into your life).

> 3) Drink it like a swan separates milk from water. (Translation: take away only the aspects of what's given that work for you specifically).

In case you're wondering, yes, all advice given in yoga teacher training sounds vaguely like it was on the b-roll for Yoda's Jedi training. (Not really, but it's fun to pretend.)

The main point is nobody knows what will work for you except for you. And you may not know what will work for you until you think it over or give it a try. Whether you're learning from a professor, a prophet, a doctor, or from me, it's all about context and fitting concepts into your life in a healthy way.

Practice Makes Perfect

I refer a lot in this book to practice. That's because, in my experience, you don't just fall into the mindset you're looking for, even if you did get a momentary glimpse at it. As with everything else in life, there is upkeep. We learned to believe terrible things about ourselves from practicing, and it takes practice to unlearn them. Whether it's reshaping our thoughts, establishing a practice of gratitude, embracing our identity through style, exercising, or meditating, it takes intentional effort to see ourselves and the world the way we want.

Practice can look like a lot of different things, from journaling to meditation to scheduled reminders to think of something positive to consciously deciding to open up to someone else. The one thing it almost always looks like is something that's difficult for you to do. You will probably have to force yourself to do your practices a lot of the time, even if you enjoy them.

If it helps, I had to set up a lot of external supports for my practices, whether that was telling my friends or counsellor about it and asking them to hold me accountable or setting explicit reminders on my phone. These days, my practices have evolved but the challenge of sticking to them is still real. Practice is hard. But you can do it!

Chapter 2 - Why Self-Worth is Hard to Find

"It's an amazing thing to say, 'I'm beautiful', without feeling like you're cocky." - Christina Aguilera

It's hard for a lot of people to say the words "I am worthy of awe" without an embarrassed laugh and a qualification or moment of defence. You know what I'm talking about. Those little things we add on to avoid making a definitive statement: "I am a good friend, I guess;" "I am a pretty decent cook;" "I can sometimes get a job done;" or "My hair is definitely on point today, but I can't speak for the rest of me." If there's no caveat, then it's probably delivered with over-the-top faux self-esteem: "Yeah, I'm the best!" This is an offshoot of the "Woo Me" syndrome, typically characterized by a person who dresses and acts loud ("Woo!") in order to attract attention, thereby compensating for the insecure little birdie they are hiding deep inside.

Challenge most people to make an unqualified statement of their value as humans and they back away quickly. There are two reasons I think this occurs. Number one: deep down in our hearts, we don't actually think we're worthy of awe, and therefore saying it with any kind of sincerity is incredibly uncomfortable. Number two: we are terrified of seeming to be conceited. We don't think we're great, and we *certainly* don't want other people to think that we would be so audacious as to think we were great.

This type of valuation of one's self, although it's just basic self-esteem, is considered one of the worst things for a person to possess.

all see the sneers and hear the eye-rolled "Oh, they are so full of themselves!" comments in our heads, and they terrify us. So much, in fact, that we don't even really want to try to believe in our value, because what if we are perceived as being conceited in the process? It's like we think gaining some real self-esteem will transform us into a stereotype who spends too much money on weird fresh-off-the-runway clothing, is mean to customer service representatives, talks about themselves constantly, and has a servant to carry around their lip balm.

So we avoid the question. We may allow ourselves to recognize one or two remarkable qualities that we possess, but anything more encompassing than that and we're finding polite excuses to visit the loo.

What Self-Worth is Not

The truth is that knowing you are a person worthy of awe does not mean you are being conceited— not in the least. Remember, our value as humans has nothing to do with our achievements, and even less to do with our looks and lifestyle. We are enough, complete, and lovable, just as we are—without any of those outward accoutrements.

People who value themselves don't need to talk about how great they are all the time. They might share great news with you because they are excited and want you to be a part of their lives, but they aren't trying to brag or bolster a sad, shrivelled heart. They are also not blind to their own faults: nobody's perfect, and nobody understands this in a healthier way than the person who is comfortable with who they are.

To look at it from another angle, take a moment to think about your friends. I am sure that you think they're wonderful, right? Of course you do! Otherwise, why would you be friends with them? Do you think they're perfect? Not in a million years! They probably have loads of faults. For example, some of my closest friends (all incredible people) have the following faults, selected at random as to avoid finger-pointing: talking way too loud (I do that too), inability to handle finances, pushiness, a total disregard for other peoples' belongings, flakiness, crippling insecurity about their bodies that comes up all the time, perpetual lateness, needing to be right every single time, a judgmental attitude, and an inability to accept help from others.

Looking at that list, you might think that I have terrible friends. No way. These are some of the best human beings I have ever met in my life. Key words: human beings. They have faults. The difference is that I spend very little time thinking about their faults. Every once and a while Friend C will be really pushy and it will annoy me. Maybe they'll annoy me enough that I need to vent about it a bit. Maybe so much that I need to say something to them about it because it's starting to make me resent them. Then guess what? I probably learn something I've been doing that was hurting them, we both deal with it, and we move on.

What I don't do is look for opportunities to see that pushiness, wallow in it, think about it over and over again, predict future pushiness, or generally endure or support that trait. I don't label or judge them as a pushy person in my mind. I see this one trait, when it arises, as one of many traits this person has, most of which are wonderful. If I do start seeing the pushiness all the time, then that's a sign that something's wrong in my relationship with that person.

This tendency to see the good in people we like is a sort of cognitive spin we put on things, linked to something called confirmation bias. Basically, confirmation bias means that once we decide on a belief, our brains start to look for evidence that confirms that belief and disregards evidence that contradicts it, mostly because it makes for easier thought processing (our brains are always looking for shortcuts to save energy). This means when you like someone and think they are lovely, you are more likely to see and remember their lovely traits than their annoying or damaging traits. On the flip side, when you don't like someone, you will tend to notice all their worst traits first. You will be generally annoyed by the things they do, and any good behaviours will seem like the exception to their awfulness.

The same logic applies to how you think about yourself. If you think that you are lame, boring, or not really all that likeable, you will only see evidence that confirms that belief and wind up intentionally blinding yourself to your inherent worth as a human.

What Self-Worth Is

Self-worth may boil down to a simple principle, reversed: do unto yourself as you would do unto others. We forgive our friends for their shortcomings and embrace their mixture of personality traits and foibles, don't we? This journey towards valuing ourselves is, in large part, one of learning how to do the same for ourselves. Imagine if you thought of yourself as a friend!

It's quite likely that right now the best you can do is recognize that you probably "should" value yourself, warts and all. It might sound like something that other people would say or that makes academic sense, but you just can't believe it. I get it. Nothing rings more false to the ears of someone who is weighed down by self-loathing than a statement of their worth. That's why we have to practice and teach ourselves to believe the truth.

At this point, you may be tempted to give up. It already seems too hard, and a voice in your head is convincing you that it doesn't even matter. If it won't change the material realities of your life, what is even the point? Even if it did work, it wouldn't change much of anything, and when it doesn't work, you'll just feel worse.

That voice is the one we're trying to learn how to shut down. Call it the darkness, a troll, your inner monster, any label that helps show you that it is unhelpful. It only sounds like the truth because you've been listening to it for so long. It's familiar and tricks you into thinking it's making you safer.

Learning to value myself, in many ways, came from learning to differentiate this voice in my mind, learning to ignore it and to choose different voices to listen to, like the voices that see the good in me and recognize my inherent value. The voice that can say "I am a creature of awe," and know that it's true.

Call that voice whatever you want—your true self, Glinda the Good Witch, the light, whatever. It is there, waiting for you. Because you are beautifully and wonderfully made.

Chapter 3 – Changing Our Minds

"Our thoughts prepare us for the happiness or unhappiness we experience" - Hazrat Inayat Khan

Here's a statement that I've hated ever since I first heard it: "It's all in your head." It usually comes from a well-intentioned person trying to comfort someone's anxiety, depression, or self-doubt. I hate this phrase. It is so casually dismissive, as though a person's pain, worry, or fear can magically disappear with the knowledge that their very real—perhaps even paralyzing—feelings are illegitimate because they exist in their head.

Well of course, it's in my head! Everything is in my head! Everything I experience becomes a part of me through the filter of my brain and its perception. That's what makes me the person I am. Yes, it's all in my head, and if what is in my head is skewing the way I experience my one and only life (or at least the only life I am currently aware of), then that is a big deal, and I want to do something about it rather than being made to feel like my concerns don't matter.

I was recently referred to Candace Pert on this topic. She is a neuroscientist who wrote *The Molecules of Emotion* and discusses current research on how our emotional experiences write themselves in our bodies. According to her research, which began with a groundbreaking discovery of our brains' opiate receptors as a graduate student, emotions are more than chemicals in our brains: they are electrochemical signals that reach every cell in our bodies. In *The Molecules of Emotion*, she writes, "As our feelings change, this mixture of peptides travels throughout your body and your brain. And they're literally changing the chemistry of every cell in your body." This means that everything really is all in our heads—and our bodies.

Another (related, but different) pet peeve is when people say, "I'm not a pessimist; I'm just a realist." I would like to respectfully disagree with the notion that the negative aspects of this life are more "real" or should be offered more legitimacy than the positive ones. To me, the good and the bad in life are equal in their depth, truth, and reality. Our interpretation of ourselves, our lives, and the world are what make life good or bad. If you ask me, life is too short to spend extra time hanging around with thoughts that make it crappier. Which is why we will begin this journey towards finding our self-worth by examining our thoughts.

We all have nasty thoughts floating around in our heads: we criticize ("You look like a foolish jerk"), condemn ("You are deeply unloveable"), and disparage ("It's not even worth trying, you always get it wrong.") These thoughts create the lens through which we have chosen to see the world. They colour everything. The events of life are going to happen no matter what, but if you decide that the bad is more real than the good, then that will become your reality, because your worldview is, indeed, all in your head.

Cognitive-Behavioural Psychology: A Brief Introduction

Cognitive behavioural psychology (CBP) is a school of psychology that examines the relationship between our thoughts, feelings, and behaviour. You may have heard it referred to as cognitive-behavioural therapy (CBT). The two terms refer to the same principles, the main difference being that CBP is more focused on the academic study of this relationship, whereas CBT refers to specific therapeutic practices.

The basic theoretical framework is pretty simple: thoughts drive feelings, feelings drive behaviours, and behaviours reinforce thoughts. So when we think "I am useless," we then feel bad about ourselves and our abilities, and then are more likely to behave in a way that reinforces this concept, by either making mistakes because we're distracted with our negative thoughts or because we are paying closer attention to those mistakes. This, then, gives us another reason to think that we are useless.

Some people have criticized CBP for being too simplistic, saying that it doesn't take into account the complexity behind issues like depression and anxiety. While this may be true, it's a practice and a line of thinking that has really worked for me. I can say, without reservation, that I love it, and many of the tools I use are hacks of this concept. Cognitive-behavioural therapies also outperform many other therapies in empirical studies (for example, Butler et al.'s 2006 "The empirical status of cognitive-behavioural therapy: A review of meta-analyses").

Even feelings that come from major life events exist only because of our interpretations (or thoughts) of those events. A promotion at work may bring you joy if you are excited about the idea of advancing your career, taking on more responsibility, or embracing a challenge; however, the same promotion may bring you anxiety or feelings of inadequacy if you are not confident in your ability to do the job or are intimidated by the new team you would be working with. A relationship ending may bring you sadness if it's an unexpected turn of events involving a person you love; on the other hand, it may bring you relief if the relationship has been weighing on you.

In CBP, not only do our interpretations and beliefs drive our feelings, but they create reinforcing cycles: say I thought my friends didn't really like me or wanted to hang out with me. That would make me feel unwanted and sad. Then, because I feel unwanted and sad, I don't reach out to see what people are doing on the weekend, and I begin to contribute less to conversations in general. Why would I, if no one wants me there? They sure don't want to hear what I have to say, right? Of course, most people are very perceptive to social cues, and so, as I retreat from engaging with my friends, they are likely to respond in kind, assuming that I don't really want to be there since I'm not participating. Suddenly, I become less likely to get invited to do things. This, in turn, confirms my belief that they didn't like me in the first place. And so the cycle continues.

These thought-feeling-behaviour cycles can go on indefinitely, and they probably will if left unchecked.

Feelings vs. Beliefs

Before we go any further, I must provide a vital word of caution: This is not a philosophy in the style of *The Secret* that is a sneaky way of blaming people for the crappy things that happen in their lives, nor is it a method to avoid every unpleasant emotion that arises. (Sorry if you like *The Secret*, but while I think there is value in focusing on the things you want in life, I can't stand by the victim-blaming.) Just because you have an aspect of influence over your feelings does not make it all your fault if you feel like crap. Blame helps no one, and sometimes you're going to feel lame, and you have to let that lame feeling exist without trying to stuff it down or beat it to a pulp with positive affirmations.

Bad feelings are unpleasant, but they are not necessarily bad things in and of themselves. All feelings are temporary, and so ignoring or quashing the unpleasant ones and desperately seeking out the pleasant ones is kind of useless. It's the beliefs and thoughts behind the feelings that matter, and your response to them should depend on what they are and where they come from.

For example, if you're feeling low because you no longer have a person that you love in your life, regardless of the circumstances surrounding the loss, then those are feelings not to be run, drill-sergeant style, out of your life. They are legitimate and important.

Sadness, loneliness, anger, impatience, anxiety, fear, uncertainty—those feelings are all going to come up sometimes because they are all part of life. If you shove them away, your poor little soul will be left high and dry, stuck with a bunch of feelings that it doesn't know what to do with. The feelings won't go away, instead choosing to pop up at unexpected times or creating further emotional block-ages in the future. If you make space for them, on the other hand, you can find peace.

I should know. Once I had moved through the hardest parts of my depression, I was terrified of bad feelings, certain that any one of them would pull me back down into the abyss. My solution was to pretend they didn't exist. It didn't work. My most recent coun-selling experience, as a matter of fact, was focused mainly on learn-ing to allow myself to a) feel those bad feelings without trying to force them away; and b) to let other people see me in those bad places from time to time. (Vulnerability! It's really hard!)

The other side of the unpleasant-feelings coin is, of course, the set of feelings that you don't need to feel. The ones that come, perhaps, because you are reliving a negative experience over and over, having an imaginary conversation with someone who once hurt you as in an attempt to perfectly articulate how they wronged you. Or maybe you are simply reminding yourself of your worthlessness, over and over. This I have heard referred to as "polishing your pain", which brings to mind an image of Gollum hunched over his precious ring—not exactly a vision of a creature at peace with himself or his life choices.

The thoughts could also be shame-spiral-type negative lies about yourself, which aren't based on anything except your imagination deciding how other people feel about you and then finding evidence for that belief.

The difference between feelings that need to be given space and feelings that are killing us is their source. After my last break-up, I needed to learn to allow myself to feel the sadness and rejection of having loved someone who didn't love me, to ugly-cry alone on my couch, and to reach out to people I love and trust for support, maybe even letting them see me and my ugly tears.

On the other hand, when I was going through life telling myself that I was worthless and unlovable, the negative feelings that came with that were completely unnecessary because they were grounded in nothing but terrible lies. I was not grieving a life circumstance but believing horrible things that made me feel worthless. In this

case, the only use these feelings had was as an alarm system, pointing to the false beliefs that were feeding them.

This is the world where, in my experience, the tools of cognitive
behavioural therapy (CBT) are best used. CBT tools are particularly useful in combating deeply held, terribly-untrue beliefs we've
learned to tell ourselves, and in letting go of the past pains we have
been polishing.

So when you have a feeling that punches you in the gut, look at its
source. Is it a truth, or a lie? If it's a lie, then you can punch it right
back. If it's a truth grounded in circumstances, well, it's best to feel
that pain and to share it with someone you trust. If you feel that
there are things you are doing that contribute to painful circumstances that you would like to try to change, you may want to check
out chapter 12, but I would recommend starting with finding some
love and acceptance for yourself first.

Reversing the Negative Cycle: A Step-by-Step Guide

I'm assuming that, if you're reading this book, you don't necessarily
feel confident about your worthiness as a human being. So how
do we interrupt a downward cycle of self-destructive thoughts and
replace it with an upward spiral that helps awaken us to our own
worth?

Step One: Identify your particular brand of damaging thoughts.

The first thing you need to do is identify the lies you are telling
yourself that are preventing you living as your wonderful self. I've
just finished telling you about some of mine.

The brand of thoughts we're looking here for sound something like "I can't do anything," "Nobody will ever love me," or "I am a terrible person." They are global, permanent statements about you as a person, as opposed to temporary, specific statements about something you did. It's the difference between "I feel bad about bombing that test" (specific, temporary) and "I am a hopeless idiot" (global, permanent).

Specific negative thoughts aren't pleasant but aren't the end of the world. They can get you on track to change behaviours you want to change (like, say, studying more next time).

Global, overarching, permanent negative thoughts about who you are as a person, on the other hand, are incredibly damaging. Part of how I always know I'm on the right path in identifying these damaging thoughts is if they sound silly or embarrassing to admit out loud. Telling someone else that I did something stupid is one thing, but telling them that I find myself completely unlovable feels kind of ridiculous when said out loud; once a thought like that is out in the open, it loses its power if for no other reason than the fact that it sounds a bit dramatic. That helps me to see it for what it really is: a lie that I have told myself so many times that it sounds like the truth.

It's powerful to see these thoughts with greater clarity and objectivity. The overarching, permanent, global negative thoughts we carry in our heads are dangerous because they are so broad and deep: they attack us at our very cores and restrict our ability to see ourselves clearly or believe in our own value beyond their rigid constraints.

My friend and pastor, Lance Odegard, once said, "the voices that shout the loudest can't be trusted." This is a good reminder for all of us, I think. If it's screaming through your mind, it's probably suspect, and worthy of examination.

Step Two: Replace those crappier-than-thou thoughts with something more in tune with how wonderful you are.

Your negative thoughts about yourself turned into beliefs because your brain practiced thinking them over and over again. Once you recognize them for what they truly are, you can move towards stopping them and replacing them with thoughts and beliefs that are not only more positive, but more accurate about your worth as a person.

The first step towards replacing negative thoughts with more productive ones lies in stopping the negative thoughts in their tracks. A good friend of mine actually says "STOP" in her mind when she recognizes a negative thought. Another friend will realize he's doing it and then distract himself by listing off all the capital cities he can think of. Anything to break the cycle.

Once the thought has been interrupted, you need to replace it quickly. There are three key things you want from your replacement thought: it needs to be specific, positive, and true.

Specific, because I have found that when responding to a legion of oft-rehearsed and well-established negative beliefs and examples about how no one loves me with a mousey, general statement like "but I am lovable," it is very ineffective. Far more effective is a concrete, specific statement, especially one involving an example. Something like, "I had lunch with Janine yesterday and she hugged me twice and laughed at my story about the guy on the bus, which is a sign that she likes me," or "John called me out of the blue to hang out, which he wouldn't have done if he didn't like me as a person," or even better, "Stephanie told me she loves me!"

If a specific example evades you in the moment, you can still be firm with your statement: "I am loved by family and friends," "My partner loves me," "I am valued at work." Yes, they will feel like lies. You will not believe them at first. But trust that belief will come.

If this is sounding really hard, it's because it is. Planning in advance is essential—when you're in the throes of a terrible, shouting thought spiral, it's going to be difficult to think of something that is both true and positive about yourself, let alone specific. And don't forget the follow-up! Negative voices are very clever, well-practiced, and might respond with something like "Janine just felt obligated to laugh but she was faking it, and she only hugged you because you hugged her," or "John hasn't spoken to you in months; that was a pity call." To those thoughts, you have to shut them up and shut them down. Plan your retorts as well. Remember: most people are busy and don't go out of their way to give hugs or compliments for no reason. Yes, you can assume everyone's lying, but that is a sucky way to live. Besides, why would *everyone* gather together to trick you into thinking you're a worthy person? That is a huge time investment from a lot of people. I realize it feels like you are inventing things when you tell yourself that they really do care, but you are already inventing things when you decide that they don't. Better to assume they're telling the truth.

These specific positive thoughts can sometimes feel as silly as the overarching negative ones. After all, they sound so elementary. Am going to use a friend hugging me as evidence against one of my most deeply held beliefs about myself? The answer is yes. And I will continue to rack up examples like that in my head until I start having too many examples of people liking me, loving me, and choosing to be around me to believe that I am fundamentally unlovable. Fundamentally unlovable people don't get greeted with smiles, get offered hugs, or anything else like that.

If you're really serious about stopping the horrible lies you've been telling yourself, then you'll just have to live with those feelings of silliness for a while. Plan some positive, true, and specific affirmations that get right to the heart of whatever makes you feel the worst about yourself, and use them. You don't have to say them out loud; no one needs to see the silliness if you don't want them to. It's worth it.

Step Three: Keep at it.

What you are doing is breaking a habit. Breaking any habit is difficult and can feel unnatural, especially when you've operated a certain way for years, maybe decades. That is why your new thoughts may feel like lies when really they are not.

It is my opinion that thought patterns can be stronger and more rigid than any other behavioural pattern. Maybe it's just because we can practice thoughts way more quickly and easily than most behaviours can be practiced. Think about the amount of time it takes you to think "I'm worthless." It happens so fast you barely even notice it, right? Compare that to the amount of time it takes you to try to change a physical habit and retrain yourself to brush your teeth the right way because your dentist just told you that you have been eroding your gums for years with a poor technique get two or three times a day to practice that physical h... ..., while you can think something terrible a thousand times a day and barely notice.

Once your brain gets used to thinking about something (in this case, yourself) in a certain way (in this case, mean-spiritedly), it becomes really hard to make changes. It's like those neural pathways are carved out of the same stones as those ancient aqueducts that just refuse to crumble. Because of this, it can be a long and arduous process to change your thoughts. However, with dedication, you will see results. It's just like trying to teach yourself to write with your non-dominant hand. At first, it feels weird, wrong, stupid and frustrating. You just want to go back to using your dominant hand because that's what is normal. It feels safe and easy because it's familiar. Stick with it. (Not the hand-changing, that is generally pointless: the thought-changing.)

Sometimes we can cling to the lies because they feel safe and familiar. Believing in yourself and trusting others is risky. We build up walls of self-loathing for a reason. One of those reasons is that they *feel* like they keep us safe. That is another lie. Sure, the walls mean you are unlikely to be disappointed by someone else not loving you or reacting as you hoped, but you are left in a terrible, dark cage. It's not a worthwhile trade.

Step Four: Get by with a little help from your friends

It is quite possible that you can't think of anything good about yourself to use for this exercise. I had a lot of trouble thinking good things about myself for a long time. In fact, if ever asked to do so, usually as an exercise from a teacher or counsellor, I would just try to think of things that I thought they might want to hear. I remember at a parent-teacher interview in grade seven, I was asked to tell my teachers which subjects I felt like I was doing well in. I didn't think I was doing well in anything; I just made sure to list one class from each of them, so that none of my teachers would feel left out. Let this be evidence to you of how blatant our inner lies can be: I was a straight-A student through (almost) my entire academic life, and I thought so little of myself I didn't believe I was doing well in *any of my subjects.*

So then, my dears, if you honestly can't think of something awesome about yourself, this could be a good time to call in some backup: your friends. That's right, I am suggesting that you ask your friends why they like you.

Yes, I have done this, and yes, it was ridiculously embarrassing. Not only did I have to tell my friends that I was seeing a therapist, something that objectively shouldn't be embarrassing but sometimes is, especially when you first get started, I then had to ask them why they liked being my friend.

Here's a fun fact: someone who doesn't like themselves, and believes that their friends don't really like them either, is probably going to find it absolutely terrifying and presumptuous to ask said friends why they are liked. It's kind of an awkward situation. Awkward, but incredibly valuable.

The responses I got from my friends were incredibly helpful. My friends were (and continue to be) truly amazing. They told me straight up why they loved me without making fun of what I was doing. There were some differences among the things each of them brought up as well as some common themes that they all mentioned. Unexpectedly, many of the things they said they liked about me were the very things that I had always envied in other people, characteristics that I aspired to possess. You can't underestimate the value of knowing exactly why the people you care the most about love you.

A few tips, should you decide to try this (which you totally should!):

1) Choose your confidantes wisely. Just because you're friends with someone doesn't mean they're the best person to help you out with this particular task. You're about to put yourself in a super vulnerable place. Make sure you feel safe with them.

2) Keep the numbers small. Even if you have a lot of friends who you trust and want to hear from, start with a handful of nearests and dearests.

3) Use email to make your request. First of all, it saves you having to make this awkward, vulnerable request face-to-face in real time and it gives you time to choose your words carefully. It also gives your friends the time to really think about their answer and craft their response. Having a written copy also means you will have a record of their response to look back on as many times as you need to.

4) Make up any excuse you want for making this request. This isn't a test of your bravery and honesty, this is a fact-finding mission for reasons why you are lovable. If you are less embarrassed by telling them that you are doing this because a therapist, teacher, parent, or alien is making you, then do so.

5) Don't ask your family. Not that family can't be loving, supportive, and helpful, but in this situation, it is far more beneficial to find out why the people who have chosen to make you a part of their lives love you, not why the people who are involuntarily connected to you love you.

I realize that this whole idea of replacing bad thoughts with good thoughts may seem pretty elementary, reductive, and ineffective. It is way more complicated than that, right? Well, it is... and it isn't. Sure, life and human beings are complex, and there are a lot of factors that can go into any situation. Making your crappy feelings too complex, however, only results in giving them unnecessary amounts of power over your life. Boiling the lies down to their most basic, changeable parts gives you back the power to make those changes, take control, and discover the extraordinary person that you truly are.

Remember, however, that the goal here is not to take every single negative thought out of your life. Some negative thoughts are useful, like the "I shouldn't have yelled at my girlfriend," thoughts that help motivate you to make healthy changes to your behaviour. Some are necessary, like actually experiencing grief. If you force your way out of that, you aren't doing yourself any favours. All you end up with is an extended processing period and anger toward yourself for having feelings you don't want, because the feelings will still be there.

This isn't about erasing all the sadness and negativity from our lives. It's about identifying the difference between "I bombed that test" and "I am a total failure," or "I feel an emptiness without this person in my life" and "My life is worthless without this person."

One has value, the other is a lie. The lies need to be banished and replaced with truth.

Chapter 4 - Feeling the Feelings

"But feelings can't be ignored, no matter how unjust or ungrateful they seem." -Anne Frank

I have talked about the importance of actually feeling your feelings already (if they aren't based in lies), but I feel this deserves to get pulled out a little more directly, because, like many things, it can be a bit more complicated.

We, as humans, have a tendency to push away the bad feelings and cling desperately to the good feelings as much as possible. Intuitively, this makes perfect sense: bad feelings feel bad. Good feelings feel good. Of course, we would rather feel good more often than we feel bad. (This basic principle doesn't always apply, of course. People living with depression sometimes feel more comfortable with negative feelings because they feel more safe or real, and so spend time pretending the good stuff isn't really there.)

The problem that arises with this is that it can lead us to live in a state of denial about our bad feelings (while they bubble down below the surface, still making their presence known), and over-identify with and grasping at the good feelings. Since feelings are transient and ever-changing, this is a bit of a dangerous way to live.

A better way might be to recognize a few things. One is that you are not your emotions. However powerful they are, however much it seems like you will never feel another way again and they have eclipsed your identity, they haven't. You are still you, no matter how you feel, and your feelings can't actually be shoved into a tiny box and thrown away.

Anyone who's ever worked in customer service has encountered irrationally angry customers: the ones who yell and call names and bang their hands on the counter and ultimately seem to overreact to everything. The first thing they teach you about dealing with these customers is that they generally just want to be heard. They have had a bad experience and even if they know that you personally had nothing to do with it, you are the face they have encountered and they need you to listen to and validate their feelings and experience.

If you have been in a situation like that, or any other where you are dealing with someone who is over-the-top upset, you may have noticed how they can almost instantly calm down once their experience is honoured. You didn't necessarily have to tell them they were right, give them their money back, or do anything else but listen to them and respond with empathy and understanding.

You may have noticed the same reaction in yourself when dealing with others. Maybe it was the last time you tried to call your phone provider, internet company, or any other large corporation's helpline. Sometimes it's a harrowing experience where you feel you have to battle everyone along the way, explaining your situation over and over as you are passed along the chain of command, all in between 20-minute holds while a recorded voice tells you they "value your patronage." You may be feeling your back tense up and your stomach clench just thinking about it. I know I am.

Then, all of a sudden you get ahold of someone who listens and understands what you're saying. Who empathizes with your frustration and apologizes where necessary. All the tension leaves your body. You can breathe again. You don't have to fight anymore; you are actually valued.

Now think about this in terms of how you treat your own emotions and experiences. The ones that come back to you time and time again as you attempt to completely ignore their existence. The ones that haunt your mind as you fall asleep at night. They are that irate customer, and every time you hold your breath to stop from crying and shove the feeling aside, you've just put them on hold and started playing obnoxious recorded promotions in their ear. You might be afraid that if you let yourself feel them, they will overpower you, but I believe you are stronger than you think. If you don't let those feelings have their time, they will never relax. Instead, they'll just form into a hardened ball inside of you.

I realize that this might sound contradictory to the cognitive behavioural work I discussed in the last chapter, but bear in mind that CBT is best used to combat the terrible lies you believe about yourself. It is not a tool for avoiding your feelings.

Recognize that Your Feelings Exist in the First Place

This leads to a basic meditation practice I learned in my yoga teacher training, where you simply observe your emotions as an interested, but unattached, onlooker. The simple mantra is to name the emotion as present: "Anger is present," "Sadness is present," "Frustration is present," "Happiness is present." Ultimately, the idea is that you will learn in, an ongoing way, that you are not controlled by your feelings, and that when more powerful emotions come along, you will have enough practice doing this that they will not overcome you.

There is value to be found in this practice, as it reinforces that your emotions are not the same as your identity. I have noticed, however, that it can also cause me to separate my brain and body—to cut myself off from my experiences. While I want to be aware that my feelings are not the key ingredient that makes up my identity, I also have come to realize that I need to truly experience my emotions to go through them, and I find that this practice sometimes helps me deny them more than experience them. So it is a valuable practice, but not, for me, a complete solution to engaging with my feelings. Sometimes, I need another technique to experience my feelings in a safe way.

Experience Your Feelings in a Safe Way

Recently I came across a complementary practice, where you both recognize and also enter into your feelings. It is outlined in great detail and explanation in the book *Perfect Love, Imperfect Relationships* by John Welwood. In this practice, you identify, feel, and enter into your emotions in a conscious way, allowing yourself to experience them.

The basic practice is this:

1) Identify the feeling/fear

The first thing you need to do is get to the core of your feeling. Starting with "crappy", "sad", or "lonely" is a good beginning. But then look at the why. Not the story of why you feel that way right now, but the longing or grief that's behind the story. Usually, it boils down to a desire for love and acceptance.

For example, if I did this exercise when I was feeling particularly down about the fact that my last boyfriend never truly loved me, never even opened up to the possibility of loving me, I could have identified the question of "why don't you love me?" which could have deepened into the question "will anyone love me?" and the desire to be seen and loved for who I am.

Once you settle on something that feels like it's hit the core, move on to step two.

2) Find the physical experience

Our emotions hold a physical place in our bodies. If you don't believe me, pay attention the next time you feel anything in a strong way. Where do you feel it? It's often somewhere in your chest or gut, although I feel things in my neck and brain sometimes. How does it feel? Sometimes it's an ache, a void, a tightness, or a heaviness, or if it's more positive, it could be an expansion, a lightness, or a bubbling over.

Identify where you are feeling things right now, and put a word on it. Touch the place with your hand. Sit with it for a moment.

3) Hold the feeling and give it space

Now that you've found it, give the feeling some space. Imagine you are holding it closely and warmly, but not squishing it. That it is embraced without being suffocated. Maybe the edges will soften a bit, but don't try to embrace it away. Let it be. Accept its presence there.

4) Enter into it

Now is the part that sounds terrifying and is also a little tricky to explain: enter into the feeling. Imagine yourself entering it, and let it surround you and fill you up. Don't worry, it will not take you over. Part of the beauty of this practice is finding that you can experience your feelings fully without losing yourself, because you are doing it with intention and consciousness.

You may begin to feel a warmth, acceptance, or love as you accept and enter into your feeling. You may not. What you will find is that the experience can be there, it can be real, you can be immersed in it, and yet, you will not drown. You will not become the feeling.

5) Exit the feeling

When you are ready, bring your awareness back to the rest of your body. Wiggle your fingers and toes. Feel how the whole rest of your body has experienced this moment. Do whatever feels good: stretch a bit, roll your neck, slump back in your chair, whatever. Then bring your awareness into the room you are in and open your eyes. You're back!

I highly recommend that you check out Welwood's book for a fuller explanation of the practice, although dabbling certainly won't hurt you.

If this meditative practice sounds like a bit too much for you right now, that's okay. You can also just let yourself feel. Alone or with someone you trust, go through the first few steps: identify the feeling and what real desire is at its root, identify where you feel it in your body and give that a name, then hold space for it. Cry, laugh, yell, whatever. Watch out if you start to tell yourself lies in the process—you are welcome to cry over the fact that you are afraid no one will ever love you, but you are not welcome to remind yourself you are unloveable.

See the difference? One is about a feeling, the other is reinforcing a belief.

Chapter 5: Gratitude

"Piglet noticed that even though he had a very small heart, it could hold a large amount of Gratitude." - A.A. Milne (Winnie the Pooh)

There is no magic pill in life to change your perspective and make everything better. If I could choose one magical ingredient in that non-existent pill, however, it would be gratitude. If you ask me, gratitude is the closest thing to mind-sorcery that exists today, and it remains a massively important key for me to combat all the dark junk that circles around my brain. In fact, if you stop reading this book right now, you now have a take-home message: gratitude can work almost instantaneously to transform your mood and your outlook on life. (Please note, I did say *can*: nothing is definite, nothing is always, and we are individuals with our own needs). People have been saying, "count your blessings" since the dawn of time for a reason, and if you take that saying literally, you will be overwhelmed with how many things you have to be grateful for.

There were a number of things that caused me to start thinking about gratitude and taking it more seriously as a practice to incorporate into my life. My mom, throughout my entire life, has been pointing out the positive side of things, so that had to have planted a seed. I was also given M.J. Ryan's book *Attitudes of Gratitude* during Christmas 2009, and right around the same time read a blog post written by a friend about her annual practice of reviewing all her successes and blessings from the past year, and then thanking the people involved.

These two influences went to work on my mind during what could be considered a generally crummy time. Right on the heels of my first-ever breakup, I had made it through the Christmas season thanks to a box of wine. I was also so broke that I couldn't really afford to do anything but sit in my dark, low-ceilinged basement suite drinking that wine and watching TV. It seemed the one small blessing in my life was that despite cancelling my free trial of cable months earlier, trashy reality shows were still being magically piped into my home.

As I've already mentioned, this first-ever relationship that preceded my first-ever breakup was the source of my first moment of clarity about my worth as a person. While that is true, my first intentional practice of worthiness hadn't quite happened yet, and there were still a lot of crummy feelings to deal with. Gratitude is the thing that kicked off my intentional journey into feeling better.

So there I was, sitting in my dank basement suite, watching trashy reality TV and scanning through my blog feed, when I came across my friend's gratitude post. Right then, at that moment, in the middle of a funk that had kept me sitting in front of the TV with my laptop for hours already, I made a little list of the awesome things that had happened that year.

Just to recap, that was the year I had been financially struggling and consistently overworked, moved from a well-lit apartment I hated to a dark basement apartment I hated, and lingered for months in a relationship that I knew was not right. After the list-making session, however, it became the year where I had finally written, produced, and performed in a play I had been sitting on for years, produced a number of other theatre events, gotten a job with real responsibility for a company that I truly loved, and had the guts to exit a relationship that wasn't working. Suddenly, 2009 went from being a sad and frustrating year to one of the best years of my life. It was a year I could be proud of, one that not only showed some of my best traits were at work but was full of a community of people who cared about and supported me.

Looking at the list, my mental energy went from a slow, crappy spiral to something much sharper and quicker. The transformation was beginning.

Next, I sent emails to everyone who had been a part of those wonderful projects to thank them for their help. That included the actors who volunteered their time to be in my plays, the friends I co-produced with, the boss who hired me despite my lack of real experience, and everyone else who had given me support. It was amazing how long the list was of people who had actually given their time and energy to things I wanted to do that year.

Taking this vital next step completed the transformation: I went from feeling kind of lonely and like a poor excuse for a human being to a loved, supported, and productive person. After all, why would so many people have gone out of their way to contribute to my life if they didn't care about me and what I was doing? It felt like someone had removed a fuzzy, too-tight swimming cap that was wrapped around my brain, finally allowing it to breathe, just a little.

It also planted the seeds of a very important perspective-shift that I am still learning to sow into my mind and heart. My life used to be about creating as long of a list of my own accomplishments as ɼ~ .e. My personal value came from what I could produce, carrying with it a heavy weight of responsibility for everything that happened. Now, I began to increasingly see life as being about contributing (a concept that feels radically different from *producing* in my mind) and about seeing the gift in everything around me. This past year, at Thanksgiving, I did some pondering on what I had to be thankful for and realized that absolutely everything I have in life is thanks to the support of someone else, at least to a degree. My life would not be the tiniest speck of what it is without the constant encounters with people who care about me and help me.

That could sound like bragging about all the people who love me, but that's not my intention. It's part of a fine balance between taking responsibility for myself and my choices and recognizing how much is out of my control and is thanks to others. For me, this helps relieve the great weight of over-achievement that tells me that my life can't have value without a giant list of accomplishments read at my funeral and reminds me that the core of life's beauty comes from meaningful contributions to (and with) people.

This new perspective wasn't the only benefit of my 2009 gratitude extravaganza, however. I wasn't just thanking people in my head. After all, I was including other people in my practice by sending little nuggets of gratitude out and into their lives.

This practice of sending gratitude to the people in my life proved to be an additional secret ingredient in my healing, for a few reasons. On a self-serving level, the act of writing each person a thank-you note forced me to think specifically about what they did that I was grateful for, giving me more time to soak in those feelings of gratitude.

More importantly, however, it also managed to brighten the days of all the people I sent notes to. Now, this should be an obvious result from the get-go, but it really didn't occur to me until I started receiving some responses to my messages over the next week. Turns out (surprise!) that getting a simple, heartfelt thank you had given these folks a lift as well, which of course, turned around and made me feel good all over again. It sounds obvious, but I think we forget how much it can mean to hear someone say "thanks."

From then on (with, of course, some falters along the way because the journey of life means forgetting and getting busy from time to time) I made a point to thank people for their awesomeness whenever possible. Once you start looking for it, you'll find things to thank people for all the time, and in the most random places. The other day I was at my friend's house and she gave me some delicious feta cheese that she couldn't eat anymore because she suddenly became lactose intolerant. Random, right? But I love feta cheese (all cheese, really—if you have some extra in your fridge, please send it my way) and getting it really brightened my day. That was totally worth an additional thank you the next day when I had delicious feta cheese in my morning eggs.

I know what you're thinking*: *this is all good, but I'm not trying to be a hippie spreading gratitude throughout the universe. I am specifically trying to feel better about myself as a human being. I mean sure, general feelings of happiness are great, but I'm trying to like myself more, not the other people in my life who seem to be doing just fine.*

Here's what I say to that:

- General feelings of happiness/joy/gratitude go a long way

in reshaping our thought patterns and are nothing to sneeze at (although why you would sneeze specifically at anything is beyond me – it sounds very rude).

- Reminding yourself of the support and love you're getting from the people around you is a reminder that you are deserving of support and love.
- Making a point of expressing gratitude forces you to look at positive things more often than negative things, a habit that just might help you when you start looking at yourself.
- Let's not be selfish. Just like a bad mood can be contagious, joy and gratitude has a way of spreading and growing too. Share it, multiply it, and dispense it freely. You'll probably feel better about yourself for having made someone else feel good.

The act of truly thanking people for a real contribution they made to your life is a thoroughly uplifting experience for everyone involved. Please do it.

*I don't actually know what you're thinking.

Chapter 6: Making Gratitude a Part of Life

"Be grateful for what you have; you'll end up having more. If you concentrate on what you don't have, you will never have enough." -Oprah Winfrey

There is more you can do with the pseudo-magical pill of gratitude than an annual practice of being thankful. This chapter connects gratitude with the work of retraining your thoughts. Using a daily practice of gratitude can help you combat your awful thoughts in an intentional way. As I mentioned earlier, you spend a lot of years training yourself to think terrible things about yourself, so it's going to take a dedicated effort to train yourself to stop.

Here's how I did it: I took a small and beautiful notebook that made me happy just to look at it, and every night I wrote down things I was grateful for that happened that day. It was a basic gratitude journal, but with a specific mission: to accumulate evidence that I was, indeed, a person of worth. Someone who was capable, interesting, valued, wanted, and loved. With such a specific, and important goal, I had to make sure I stuck with it, so I modified the traditional gratitude journal idea to fit my life and my mission.

First of all, every entry was simple and point form. I wrote a quick little bullet point about whatever the thing was that I was grateful for. No long flowery sentences about my feelings, no explanations or attempts to unpack what anything meant. Just straight-up bullet points. This was for the very practical reason of taking very little time and energy, making me less likely to stop doing it.

53

Also in the interest of saving time and energy, and thus making this into a long-lasting habit, I committed to writing only three things down a day. Usually, I wrote way more than that, but three was my minimum. That way, if I actually did have a terrible day, I wouldn't feel bad about myself for not having ten or twenty things to write down or spend half an hour agonizing over my list.

Finally, since I was specifically trying to learn to feel better about myself, and not just generally grateful, I narrowed the focus. I specifically tried to note things that I had done that I was proud of, or compliments I'd gotten from other people that made me feel good. I generally focused on things that showed that I was a valuable person on this earth.

I wanted the examples to be really specific. When I'm stuck in a dark place and convinced that no one loves me, a general statement like "No, you have friends" doesn't help. I need examples, not only that I have friends, but that I have friends who want to be friends with me. Since I could not see value in myself, I needed specific examples that other people saw value in me, and what those things were that they valued. I also needed to feel competent as a person and that the world was a generally good place, so I needed examples that helped surface those feelings.

I knew I was doing it right when the things on the list were such little, basic items that they felt kind of silly to even write down. Just like how our negative self-talk a little embarrassing and silly when spoken out loud, the weapon against it has to be on the same level.

Here are some examples of items on my list, with names removed for the purposes of saving some pride on everyone's parts:

- I ran into Acquaintance and she seemed genuinely happy to see me.
- I spent an hour writing instead of watching TV.
- Good Friend gave me a big, meaty hug when we met up.
- Coworker commented that I did a good job on today's project.
- Friend called me up of her own free will to make plans.
- I got to walk in the sunshine.
- I woke up early enough to do yoga before work.
- Met someone new and had a really nice, short conversation with them.
- The barista seemed extra friendly, and maybe was flirting?
- I had a good idea for a new project.

My list is comprised of lots of little things that seem like they should be taken for granted, but that, when you need them, come desperately in handy.

You may also notice a lot of items on my list that may look like I was getting my validation elsewhere. Well, to a degree I was. Since I saw myself as unloveable, the first step in reversing that was to see the various ways other people loved and validated me. I didn't just talk about others though—I would also note the things I had done or experienced on my own that felt validating in their own right.

A few more things to consider, should you start making lists:

1) Keep it specific. I've already said it, but it can't be emphasized enough. This is no place for the generalities of "I have good friends" or "my family is supportive." Nope. Those are nice thoughts, but what is helpful here

is a humiliating level of specificity. Specificity gives you concrete, measurable evidence for your worthiness that you can use to combat the negative thought-spirals that might come up later.

2) Be generous. If you can frame things in a positive, grateful way, then do it. Don't worry about continuity or what anyone else might think if they read it. This isn't for them. One day my list would include that I had woken up bright and early with loads of energy and accomplished a ton at work, the next day it would include that I had let myself sleep in and had a nice, relaxing morning. I could have framed day one as manic over-achievement and day two as laziness, but really both are good things to do that I can be proud of and feel grateful for.

3) Write it down, or find another concrete way to record your happy moments. Whenever I would feel too lazy to write it out and try to just think about the things I was grateful for, my mind would wander off, I would fall back into negative thought patterns, and I would be left with nothing to show for it afterwards. Having the list was great because I could give it a second glance after everything was written down to reaffirm how much I did, indeed, have to be grateful for, as well as how much evidence there was that I was a person worthy of awe.

This not only helps you change your perspective on a day-to-day level (one friend tried it too and commented that she found herself looking throughout the day for things that could go in the journal, shifting her focus to the positive), but it gives you an ever-growing arsenal of evidence that your life is full, valuable, and meaningful.

Other Ways to Incorporate Gratitude into Your Life

Maintaining a gratitude list may not float your boat. There are other ways that are equally concrete. I have one friend who uses her Facebook statuses to share gratitude. For a period of time, she makes herself think of one, or many, things that she's grateful for every day and shares it. My guess is that this creates a sense of accountability for her to continue doing it, as well as an ability to easily share her gratitude with anyone else who may have been involved in the thing she's writing about. Plus, we're all so ridiculously connected to social media these days (if we choose to partake) that it can feel easier to post a status update than grab a notebook and write something down.

Another friend started a blog where every single day, she wrote about the best thing that happened that day. The benefit of this over the point form list is that it actually turned her life into a competition of good moments: every day she would have to sit down and think not just of what was nice in her day, but determine what was the *most* awesome thing in her day. Then she would write about it in detail, reliving all the aspects of that one thing that made it so great.

Recently I read about an idea called Radical Gratitude where, in the midst of a bad circumstance, you ask yourself, "Is there anything here I can be grateful for?" It is the counterintuitive practice of being grateful, even for negative circumstances originated by Mary Jo Leddy in her book *Radical Gratitude.*

example, I was once walking to a meeting I really didn't want to attend, for a group where I held responsibilities I no longer wanted to carry. I was dreading it and thinking only about how great it would be once I left. Then I asked myself if there was anything in this situation I could be grateful for. Of course, there was: I was in a position of trust and responsibility, I was making connections and meeting new people, I was learning new processes for dealing with change and gaining leadership skills. Thinking about this didn't make me want to go any more than before, but it helped offer a slight reframing of the situation.

These days I have taken up a longer form of journal writing to process my thoughts and gratitude. I also have reminders set on my phone. A few times a day, I get a ping, and when that happens, I take a moment (and a deep breath) and think of something I'm grateful for. I like it because it spreads the gratitude out throughout my day.

The types of things you're grateful for might change over time. I recommend in the beginning that you give yourself a mission to notice the kinds of things you need to see. I needed to know that I had value to others and to myself, so I specifically looked for that kind of evidence. These days I let my gratitude flow free-form, and I welcome whatever comes up.

Whatever you do, find a way to invite gratitude into your daily life. Going back to Chapter 3, on changing your thoughts, gratitude has a wonderful way of doing that, and you can use gratitude as an intentional weapon against negative, spirally thoughts.

Plus, if you're still having trouble thinking of things about yourself that are worthy of awe, try starting here. A little gratitude goes a long way.

Chapter 7: Moving from Thoughts to Action

"How we spend our days is, of course, how we spend our lives." - Annie Dillard

In both acting and writing, a popular maxim is that a character is revealed through action. In other words, it doesn't really matter what a character says about themselves, or how the playwright or author has described them. It's what the character does that determines the kind of person they are.

What if this advice for writers and actors could apply to our everyday lives? What if the things we choose to do each day spoke to who we are as people? What if we could use that to tune into our unique worthiness?

I believe that the more time we spend doing the things that make us feel alive, that connect us to our hearts, the more we will feel alive and connected to our hearts, and the more our unique beauty will shine through in the rest of our lives.

Just to be clear, this is not about accomplishments. This is simply about taking moments, where you are able, to do things that help you feel better in incremental ways.

Yes, this is another step that seems kind of obvious—it doesn't take a fancy degree to know that you'll feel better if you do things that make you happy. Yet how many of us go straight from working to Netflix or grabbing a drink? While those activities may provide respite for our tired brains, they do little to activate or enliven our souls. You'd think doing things that you enjoy would coi.... ly, but often, self-care takes work, especially if we are more practised at beating ourselves down than listening to our hearts. With easy comforts like scrolling through Instagram or following YouTube rabbit trails at the tips of our fingers at all times, it takes real effort to choose and prioritize activities that truly nourish us.

So how do you do it? You're going to start to notice that I like step-by-step lists. I am not trying to be reductive or imply that all of life can be broken down into point-form lists, but I do think that they are a great for setting clear intentions and following through. Many things that seem big and overwhelming are easier to accomplish than we think; we just need to break them down into steps, and that's exactly what lists are good for.

As I've mentioned earlier in the book, healing and moving towards wellness takes time, and is the product of many interconnected, incremental steps that can seem invisible or even trivial. Life is like that, too; it consists of so many small moments that we might not readily think of as significant accomplishments, but those everyday actions are often the ones that catalyze the big-ticket changes in our lives. In the spirit of honouring and celebrating the small actions that make us who we are, I'm focusing this chapter on the simple steps we can take to help us feel better. And they start with making simple, non-judgemental lists.

Here's what it boils down to: 1) think of things that you want to do; 2) actually do them. That's literally all there is to it. We often trick ourselves into thinking that happiness is more complicated than that. Bear with me; I don't think it has to be.

Step One: Think of Things You Want to Do

You would expect that thinking of things we want to do should be easy, right? Unless, of course, we have spent our lives thinking of ourselves as unworthy of love, wellness, or esteem. Then we may not be very practiced at listening to our heart's desires,

When I'm asking you to think of some things that you want to do, what I'm talking about are concrete activities that feel good for you. Think about specific hobbies and extra-curriculars that you love to do and wish you would do more often, not abstract concepts or states. And by "feel good for you" I mean the kinds of things that just feel *right*. Not necessarily the easiest things, but the things where, on a large scale, you feel like you've clicked into place and your whole self is engaged and alive with the activity. On a smaller scale, they are things that always help you feel good because they help you feel more like yourself, or help you get to a place you want to be. They satisfy a little pushy ping in the back of your mind that wants to engage with life. I encourage you to make a list of those things.

My list includes making a real breakfast every morning, doing yoga, writing, bringing people together by hosting parties and events, being in nature, consuming delicious cheese and beer, singing with passion and zero concern for accuracy, learning new things, reading good books, and dancing. Notice that these are things that might be called actionable items—or, for the bigger ones (like hosting events), things that can be broken down into actionable items, things that not only can be concretely accomplished, but that require action in order to make them happen. You know if you're do-

ing it or not, and it's the process of doing them that he
victorious, energized, valuable, alive, whole, or just plain

You may already have a three-page-long list of things, and if that's
the case, great! Jump ahead to step two and start doing them. But
if you're having trouble thinking of things to do that help you feel
well, it's not because you're stupid or deficient. Maybe it's because
you've spent so much time thinking about the negative parts of
your life, you're out of practice thinking about good things. Or perhaps you live in a world with so many expectations and so much
pressure you can't separate things you enjoy doing because you genuinely love doing them and things you do because you feel like
you have to. Or maybe you're so exhausted after you fulfill all your
obligations that you feel the need to turn your brain off at the end
of the day with TV and the Internet, and so you can't remember
what turns your brain on anymore. There are so many reasons that
we might feel lost when faced with the prospect of doing things
just because we like them. I know I did.

I encourage you to practice kindness towards yourself. Don't judge
yourself for enjoying the things you enjoy, and certainly don't beat
yourself up for not having dedicated time to doing them in years
or being unsure of where to start. My hope for this process for you
is to help you cultivate new space in your life for activities that can
help bring about a new sense of spaciousness, actualization, and joy
in your life.

If you're having a hard time listing what you like to do, consider these points:

1) Try to remember the last times you felt really well—well in mind, well in body, well in spirit. What were you doing at those times? In consideration of your future self, start paying attention in your life to when you feel really good: what are you doing? Is there a common thread? Maybe it's physical activity, artistic expression, nature, or mastering a new skill. Don't worry about getting too big with this: it can be as small as moving from your bed to the couch, changing out of your pyjamas, or getting some sunlight on your face if that's where you're at now.

2) Notice the things you tell yourself or others that you would love to do if you had more time, money, or talent.

3) Take an inventory: for one week, every day, make a list of 20 things you would like more of in your life. This can be anything, from time spent outside, to chocolate, travel, stimulating intellectual conversations, or simply quiet moments. Don't look at your previous lists before writing a new one. Then, at the end of the week, review the lists and note the things that came up frequently, or that really strike a chord with you. If some are abstract concepts, find a way to tie them to a concrete activity. If you wrote down that you want more laughter, perhaps you could spend some time every day watching your favourite YouTube comedian or talk to a friend who al-

ways makes you laugh. (This exercise comes from a great book called *How to Put More Time in Your Life* by Dru Scott that has lots of great visioning/planning exercises to help direct how you use your time.)

Remember, these don't have to be big-deal things. Check out my list again: some of the items are fairly major undertakings, but most of them are small and easy to do with little preparation or energy.

Step Two: Actually Do Them

Ah, deceptive simplicity, how I love thee! I feel like a 1990's Nike commercial with this one, but really, at the end of the day, all you have to do is tear yourself away from whatever electronic device is sucking your time and energy and just do it!

"But I have so many excuses for why I don't do the things I love!" you say. "Oh really?" I respond. "What are they?" Then I bet you five million dollars you will say that you don't have time. (Note: this is not a real bet, unless you want to give me five million dollars.)

Screw that. Saying you don't have time to do something that is important to you is saying you don't have time to enjoy life. Yes, we have work and countless other life obligations that keep us running through life and land us at home totally exhausted. Some of these you simply have to do (especially if you aren't a person of "independent means," if they really exist), and some of these things you could cut out of your life, should you make the choice. Either way, there are ways to fit things into the busiest of lives.

Take, for example, a yoga practice. When studying yoga, one is encouraged to engage with their practice every day. That feels like a huge commitment that no one has time for, right? This is how my instructor taught us to manage it: if you feel like you don't have time to do yoga one day, then just roll out your yoga mat, stand at the end of it in tadasana (the basic starting pose), and then roll it up and put it away. There. You've now completed your yoga practice for the day.

Now, chances are pretty good that once you "show up" on the mat, you'll feel silly just standing there for a few seconds and then rolling it up, so you'll do a forward bend, and then maybe a full sun salutation, and then no matter how much or little you do, suddenly you're practicing the yoga you didn't have time for.

There are two nuggets of wisdom embedded in this advice. One, showing up is often the biggest hurdle. Once we get there, we often find we have more time than we thought we did. Especially for an activity that enriches our lives. Two, work with what you've got: there's no minimum level of activity required. Doing one sun salutation counts doing yoga, so you can feel good that you've taken the time to give yourself the gift of yoga that day and experience the benefits of a refreshed mind and slightly-more-limbered body.

If you tell yourself that it's only worth it to do something you really want to do if you can devote a large chunk of time to it, then you will probably never do it. If you love writing and have a crammed schedule, book 10 minutes a day and get whatever you can down in that time. If you love dancing, play one dance-party-inducing song and groove on your lunch break. If you love jogging, run around the block. If you love photography, bring your camera with you while you walk to the corner store and see what you can capture.

By fitting things in wherever you can and letting yourself enjoy and value that time where you've got it, you will inject mini-moments of wellness into your day that you can carry with you through the crazy busyness. And who knows, you might just find more time than you thought you had.

This also points to the value of a routine and structuring your life to fit in things that you want. It might sound rigid, but you aren't going to wake up in six months and find that you magically finished the painting that's been itching in your fingers if you never made time. Whether you're finding ten-minute windows or scheduling in full afternoons to do what you love, you need to plan ahead for it. You need to get the supplies you need in advance and you need to decide when you do it. Is it a lunch break activity? Is it a first thing when you wake up or last thing before bed event? Will you do it right after work? Pick a time. Start building a routine around it. After all, that time is going to pass anyway.

"Okay, okay," you say, "maybe I've got time, but I can't afford it!"

Admittedly, that one's trickier. Some hobbies are expensive. There are, however, usually low-cost alternatives. Example: some sports or dance styles require expensive equipment or lessons. Well, if you really want to do this thing, then swallow your pride and ask around if anyone has used equipment you can borrow. Check out second-hand shops or schools that might have stuff people have left behind.

If you need lessons and have a marketable skill, offer it up! Small businesses and independent contractors often love a good barter, so long as you're offering a service they actually need. You can trade piano lessons for haircuts or housecleaning, for example. Community centres are also a great place to look, and most colleges and universities offer rec programs that are both cheap and available to the public.

While you're doing all this, saving even a small amount of money from every paycheque to invest in yourself can go a long way. Or perhaps there are ways that you can turn that skill you're bartering into more money.

"FINE!" You say, frustrated that I am removing your excuses for avoiding awesomeness, "but I'm really not any good at the thing I want to do."

This is my favourite excuse, because it is actually the worst excuse. You only get better at an activity by doing it, and this is a hobby, not a career, right? Maybe you're hoping your hobby will eventually become a career, and that's okay, but that really just means that you need to work even harder at it.

We have this funny idea in our society, especially when it comes to artistic or athletic endeavours, that an inborn talent is all that matters and it's not worth doing something if you aren't naturally a rock star at it. Not true. Yes, some people seem to be born with a pre-existing proclivity towards an activity and they will naturally learn it much faster than you, but talent is unreliable and fickle. It is nothing without a strong skill set to back it up, and by practicing and working hard at the skill, you might even outshine the "naturally talented" one someday when their talent plateaus.

Everyone has to start somewhere, and the only thing you will become good at by sitting around and thinking about how other people are better than you at something is feeling crappy. Besides, we are trying to separate our sense of worth from results and enjoy the ride here. If this is something you love doing, that brings you joy and life and helps you feel good, then who cares if you're not that skilled at it? Who cares if you ever get that good at it? Just do it and feel the goodness.

Set a Goal

I have found that it can sometimes help for me to set a goal related to my activity, or set up some sense of public accountability, just because it is so easy to let the detritus of life get in the way of what I actually want to do. Let's call it the *Julie and Julia* phenomenon. If you haven't read the book *Julie and Julia: My Year of Cooking Dangerously* by Julie Powell, or seen the movie, the story centres around dear Julie, who wants to feel better about her life. She loves cooking, and sets a goal to go through Julia Child's cookbook in a year, making a blog to help her chart progress and give her a sense of accountability to stick with it.

The trick is to not tie your enjoyment of the activity to any outcome. Start a blog, but don't expect to have a book and movie deal come of it. Sign up for that half-marathon, but don't pin it all on making a certain time.

If you're not into public accountability, choose a concrete time to work your new activity into your schedule. Make it easy on your-

.ding a time that is low on distractions, and during a time here you feel most able to add a new, habitual activity into your routine.

Get Back At It

I once completely fell off the bandwagon with two of my big feel-better activities: doing yoga and writing. This fall was sparked partially by the onset of a summer when my schedule become more unwieldy, and partially by Heartbreak 2.0: The Heart Crushing Continues, also known as my second break-up. It was one that really ate my heart and I let it throw me off my game for a long time as a result. I think it took me almost a year to get back into doing yoga with any regularity. I returned by simply planning to do it and then doing it. That's it. No fancy tricks. I didn't have to justify my year of absence or make up for it with a big splashy forty-day challenge. I just did it again, and then again, and again. If I missed a day or two, then I just did it again the next day.

This should be a boost for my fellow over-achievers: while having goals, projects, and deadlines may give you a sense of purpose in your wellness journey, there is no need to beat yourself up if and when you lose track of where you're going for a while. It happens. Once you realize what you've done, dust yourself off and see if you can't find a way to bring those good activities back into your life. What's done is done, and all you can do is move forward!

The point of this chapter is not for you to set goals and lofty dreams that will add stress to your life. If you do start to feel stressed out about your activity, give yourself a break, and consider the core of why it is valuable to dedicate intentional time to doing things that help you feel well. You'll not only feel well more often, but you'll be actively creating this wellness and perhaps even joy in your life.

The beautiful thing about our lives is that we can structure them however we want. Sure, there are work schedules and other obligations that we need to work around, but whatever free time you have is yours to control. Why not spend that time doing something that helps you feel better?

Chapter 8: Looking Good

"If you retain nothing else, always remember the most important rule of beauty, which is: who cares?" - Tina Fey

"If I didn't define myself for myself, I would be crunched into other people's fantasies for me and eaten alive." -Audre Lorde

There have been at least a bazillion articles written about how to look great, and there is no way that is an exaggeration. They are always full of fun and easy-to-follow rules that are almost always geared at what will make other people think you look amazing so that they will want to spend time with you and maybe have The Sex with you.

If you read more than one of these articles, you might find them confusing, as they are also almost always contradictory: wear bright red lipstick, don't wear bright red lipstick; show off the goods, keep them under wraps; be bold and strong, be soft and supple; wear this particular brand, now wear this other brand. And why? Often they boil down to sad heteronormative thinking about how men *love* women who wear this and women *hate* it when men wear that. If they aren't lumping people into basic gender binaries with uniform tastes, then the message usually has something to do with fitting in or an aspirational lifestyle: people will never want to be seen with you unless you wear this!

Thinking about this just makes me sigh a lot, because regardless of whether or not attracting potential mates is your main concern, claiming that an entire group of people loves or hates a particular look is sort of ridiculous. It's hard enough for me to say that I love or hate a particular look *all the time*. How many times have you put on your "favourite sweater," looked in the mirror, and been instantly horrified at how terrible it looks? Or conversely, how many times have you pulled a sweater out of the back of your closet that you previously thought looked terrible and realized that you actually look amazing in it? I'm pretty sure the sweater didn't change that much since last month. What probably happened is that your taste changed—maybe drastically.

As people, we are constantly changing and growing. It's a wonderful, annoying, confusing, fun part of being human. While it may be worthwhile to examine ourselves if we are drastically changing our opinions and tastes on a monthly basis, in general, I believe it is incredibly important to embrace these changes. And while fashion and personal style may seem like frivolous elements of personal growth, the aesthetics we are drawn to and the way we choose to present ourselves are intrinsically connected to our sense of self.

I once saw an interview with Madonna on Much Music (that's the Canadian version of MTV) where she was asked if she'd ever regretted any of her many drastic looks. The answer? Every. Single. Time. Every time she changed her image, it was because she hated or regretted the last one. So if Madonna's tastes can change so quickly, and she's a fearless fashionista extraordinaire who has shaped many of the trends we've been asked to follow, how can you expect to dress a certain way to constantly please an entire segment of the population?

A much better bet is doing your hair, face, and clothes in a way that makes *you* feel like the most marvellous version of yourself. This doesn't mean spending thousands of dollars on a new wardrobe or conforming to some external definition of "marvellous." It's quite the opposite, actually. It's simply wearing things that make you feel good about yourself when you put them on, whatever that means to you. Jumping on every new trend might be fun and adventurous for you, or it might make you feel lost and like you're never quite good enough. Conversely, you might secretly feel most like yourself wearing black head-to-toe, but worry that it's too boring or monochrome.

Whatever it is that you can put on and feel comfortable and good about yourself, that is as far as your fashion rules need to go. It is worth being aware, however, that when we are used to criticizing ourselves, we might be too afraid to even consider the option of feeling good about our appearance, either because we don't believe we deserve it, or because we have been telling ourselves we are ugly for so long we can't see past it.

I used to be unable to wear lipstick because I was convinced that people would look at me and wonder, "Who does she think she is, wearing that lipstick? She looks like an ugly child playing dress up." Lipstick was for women who were fancy, put together, and beautiful. In my mind, wearing lipstick spoke of confidence: you had to see yourself as a certain level of attractive in order to wear it. I certainly did not see myself as anything close to attractive, and thus I never wore lipstick unless someone else made me. So if you're reading this and thinking, "What if I actually look like a disaster and don't realize it? Remember that time I put on my favourite sweater and realized it looked hideous? Because I remember that time and it makes me doubt every clothing choice I've made since then," I get it. So much of how we see ourselves is tied up in how we look and how we assume others see us.

In a perfect world, we would all look in the mirror, feel good about what we see, and then not care what other people think. In fact, through most of my life, people assumed this was my attitude. I spent high school dressing intentionally weird, partially because I liked it, and partially because it was very important that I be seen as a unique soul. That was a different kind of costume—sure, I liked the clothes I was wearing, and for the most part, I was being myself, but it was more of a defiant, "In your face!" to conformity than a truly genuine expression of my inner self.

Don't get me wrong: I fully embrace that we style ourselves in part with an idea of how we want other people to see us, and that means that we care at least a little bit what they think. There is a difference, however, between considering how others will see you because you want to them to perceive you in the same way you perceive yourself, and considering how they'll see you because you want them to like you more, or make them think you are like them. Things go wrong when we start altering something that helps us feel good about ourselves to satisfy what we hope other people will think is attractive.

Like it or not, we do make judgements about each other based on how we look. I don't mean judgements of value, but more like social cues that help us predict what kind of person we're dealing with. In extremes, we have the super-coifed, high-flash designer types, versus the ill-fitting, patchworked, don't-care types. While you can't value a person more or less based on these styles, you can make some guesses about their differing lifestyles, and potentially some of their values.

Most of us fall somewhere in between, with flares of the trendy, classic, artsy, hippy, alternative, or whatever else fits our personalities. At the end of the day, wouldn't you rather present yourself in a way that reflects your personality than pretend to be someone else? This bodes especially true if you're concerned about attracting others to you. No matter who you are or what your style is, there are people out there who will be attracted to you simply as you are. If you change or hide it, you might miss them and instead draw someone in who doesn't appreciate you. That's not ideal.

Basically, let's not pull a Sandy in *Grease*—you don't need to have a 180-degree makeover to make it acceptable for someone to like you. If they can't accept you with your ponytail and Keds, move on!

Chapter 9: I Need Love, Love

"Having someone wonder where you are when you don't come home at night is a very old human need." - Margaret Mead

I have spent most of my life as a single person, watching as my friends bounced from partner to partner, love to love, ultimately landing with (seeming) ease on one that stuck. It was sometimes hard to witness their uncomplicated stroll down Love Lane, as someone who wanted love of my own.

In this chapter, I will start to unpack the quirky, complex mystery that is love. Specifically, looking for love when you aren't sure you love yourself. It can be so tempting in this situation to just grab that random hand and hold onto it. Anything to save you from being alone with your own thoughts, right? Except that what we really want when we are looking for love is companionship. Someone who will see us, all of us, and choose to stick around.

Not everyone desires romantic love in their life, and if that's you, that's okay. Before you skip past this chapter, take one moment to consider: are you writing off romance because you don't think you deserve it, or is it genuinely just not something you need? If it isn't, what other kinds of companionship do you desire in your life? It's possible that you can transfer some of these principles over to non-romantic partnerships.

Finding someone, anyone, to be in your life and hold the mantle of "significant other" may satisfy a basic need to be chosen, but it also devalues your ultimate worthiness to know and be known, and to be loved wholly, for who you truly are. Being with someone just to have someone can be one of the loneliest experiences of all time. Not only is it impractical, taking you off the "market" for finding someone who you truly connect with, but it doesn't recognize your intrinsic worth. You deserve True Love, a love that deserves capital letters because it's a love that that accepts and embraces who you are and allows you to do the same for someone else. It's not a love free of struggles or hardship, and it doesn't even mean you'll never feel lonely, but it does mean that you have a partnership built on admiration, respect, attraction, and shared values.

Luckily, your worthiness for love does not depend on whether you believe in it. Unluckily, finding a healthy, supportive partnership is more difficult if you don't. While I don't agree with the truism that you can't love others until you love yourself, I do think that for a romantic relationship to be equal, balanced, and healthy, each person needs to believe that they are worthy of their partner's love. Without that belief, it is likely you will fall into traps of remaining in bad relationships, putting all your self-worth in your partner's hands, being unable put up boundaries, or abandoning everything else in your life for the sake of your significant other.

This doesn't mean that you have to wait until you reach some ineffable state of "wholeness" before you start seeking love. There is no perfect moment of readiness when your love is destined to be holy and complete. It does mean, however, that you might want to take some time to reflect on your worth, values, and needs, and to seek greater self-awareness as you embark on a journey of love.

It's not desperation—it's an actual human need!

You might feel ashamed to admit that you're lonely and craving romantic companionship. I certainly did. In a society that values the heroics of individuals who carry the weight of the world on their completely independent shoulders, it often seems like there is little room for us to comfortably, frankly discuss the fact that we are also social creatures who really need each other. So let's do an experiment and see what happens if we throw off concerns of being (or seeming) desperate for love, at least for now. After all, we are lovers at heart! The lives of lovers takes many forms. Perhaps an ideal partnership to you means getting married, having babies, and living in a house with a yard. Perhaps it more closely resembles a lifelong cohabitation in a cozy basement suite where you and your partner invest in a chosen family of friends, or maybe you are more interested in exploring polyamorous connections, sharing your love within a community that cares. Love is love, my friends.

Denying the fact that we are humans in need of love, whatever that love looks like, only serves to put you in a place of, well, denial. It reminds me of when I was 14 and decided that since boys obviously didn't like me (the first boy to ever express a romantic interest in me—he held my hand—picked someone else to be his girlfriend), I would simply not like them. As a young teenager, I was just doing what middle-aged women who go through terrible divorces do about 26 years early: swearing off men.

My resolve lasted a pretty darn long time. From then on I would more or less only admit to being "attracted" to a guy, but never to actually liking him. After all, attraction just meant I recognized he

, and I reasoned that I couldn't help that. Liking someone, ..e other hand, meant emotional investment and a hope there ˌuld be more. I refused to truly recognize any feelings I had for a fella until well into university.

Where did all this denial get me? Well, it didn't get me into a happy and healthy relationship, that's for sure. It also didn't stop me from having crushes or the drawn-out, painful bouts of longing that accompanied them. What it did mean was that while I was drowning in loneliness, I was pretending that the loneliness didn't actually exist. This meant that not only was I feeling empty and unloved, but I was punishing myself for it because I didn't think I was supposed to feel that way.

That's what denying your feelings does: instead of getting rid of them, it just slathers a layer of self-loathing and judgement on top of the pile of emotions that are still actually there.

So if you want your life to include growing old with one loving person, then admit it! If you want your life to include a varying, dynamic array of partners who dip in and out of seasons of your life, admit that, too! There's nothing wrong with it, and wanting a partner—or a variety of partners—certainly doesn't have to mean you are empty or desperate. If we were talking about career and you wanted to change jobs, nobody would say you were desperate; it would just mean that you'd feel better about your life and your work if you were doing something different for a living. So why throw piles of judgment on yourself for wanting romantic companionship?

Of course, before going too far down this path it's good to check yourself and make sure you aren't using your efforts to snag a potential partner as a Band-Aid over other bad feelings, or assuming that all your problems will go away if you find someone. They simply will not, and it's best to face them on their own instead of tangling them up here.

Seeking a temporary respite from dating or feeling an overall lack of desire for a romantic partner in your life are both normal and reasonable ways to live as well. Just to be confusing, the flipside of a society where we feel like we're being desperate if we want love is that we think there is something wrong with us if we don't. Fret not if this is you, and give yourself the gift of investing in your friends, family, career, and other joys in life.

When it comes to desperation, I am willing to bet a large sum of baked goods (because I don't have very much money) that it does matter how desperate you *feel* in your quest to find someone. It's the action of committing to someone you know isn't right for you that bears the unmistakable glow of desperation. You shouldn't have to talk yourself into loving someone and compromise your mental health and sense of self-worth in the process, nor should you have to strong-arm someone else into loving you. I have done both of these things, for two reasons: I didn't believe I deserved love, and I couldn't stand the idea of being alone with myself while I waited for it. My self-judgement also told me that nobody would choose to love me on their own, so I had to both push myself to love the first person who showed interest in me, regardless of how I felt, as well as force them to love me when they pulled away. It was simultaneously heartbreaking and exhausting.

.act is that there are plenty of emotionally stable, well-rounded, satisfied-with-life individuals who want a partner with whom to experience their emotionally stable, well-rounded, satisfying life. You just need to value yourself enough to wait for them and accept them when they are in front of you.

There is also an uncomfortable truth that few people want to admit: not everyone finds someone. Some people insist that if you are open to love and do the right things, you will find it, no matter what. In my observation of life that is true, but only when you broaden the definition of love beyond romance. When you look for other kinds of love in the world, you can see that it abounds to everyone that doesn't close themselves off to it. When you look for romantic love, I don't know why, but not everyone seems to find it. There does seem to be an amount of luck in finding a partner.

That's why an important goal, as we quest for love, is to value and respect ourselves enough to be okay with who we are no matter what, and to give ourselves the space to grieve what doesn't happen. Your worthiness of love does not depend on whether you happen to meet someone who is interested in you, someone who is healthy, stable, and open-hearted and who you feel the same way about. You are a beloved creature, no matter what.

Valuing self, valuing partnership

It can be relatively easy to find someone willing to date or marry you if that's literally all you want. There are truly desperate people out there. Remember on *Sex and the City* when Charlotte decided that she was going to find herself a husband? It was only a few short episodes later that she found and proposed to Trey, resulting in what I consider to be the worst marriage ever depicted on television, which is saying something.

Fortunately, we can learn from Charlotte's mistakes! We want our partner to be someone who enriches our lives just as much as we enrich theirs. Someone who is another equally awesome and whole person, not some half a soul looking for someone to fill them up and complete their life. (That's my subtle way of saying that this whole "soulmate" thing is bunk. I believe there are, at the very least, *several* people on this planet you could happily spend the rest of your life with, not just one. That means there are options, and you don't have to settle for a real-life Trey or despair that you will never meet your soulmate because they live across the world.)

Now, to be clear, I don't mean that you're going to meet someone and they will be ideal relationship material for you and you'll never have to work at anything because your lives will automatically be enriched by each other. What I mean can be compared easily to different kinds of friendships.

The so-called soulmate

You have some friends who you met and just clicked with. Your energies, values, interests, and other key factors felt like an instant match. You trusted each other and wanted to spend time together and you both knew it was mutual right from the get-go. Those are the closest thing we might find to soulmates in this life: people with whom we have a special connection we can't quite explain. This kind of soulmate can exist in our romantic partners, friends, relatives, or anyone else, and we aren't limited to just one.

The slow burn

Then there are the friends who you meet, get along with, and as you continue to spend time together, your relationship deepens. Slowly, they become a confidante and companion as you learn more about each other. Over time, you build a deep and meaningful friendship.

The one who just happened to be around

Finally, there are the people who you meet and, because of some circumstance, they are a part of your life. You may not dislike them, but for whatever reason you don't really connect. Maybe their values are just a tad too different from yours or they communicate in a way you don't quite get and you wind up frustrated in many conversations. Maybe your interests are completely different and there are few things for you to do together that you both enjoy. Maybe they make jokes that you know are meant as kind-hearted ribbing, but they still kind of hurt your feelings. Maybe you enjoy hanging out with them at parties and group events, but feel at a loss when you're with them one-on-one, or you simply don't quite feel comfortable enough with them to share your deeper self. Whatever the reason, they may be around, but they aren't someone with whom you want to pursue a deeper relationship.

Hopefully, it's obvious that it's the people in that final category—those who just happen to be around—who are the wrong choice for romance. The concept that dating someone just because they're around is not a recipe for lifelong bliss sounds like it should go without saying, but when loneliness, attraction, sex, and a potential for romance enter the mix it can be easy to disregard, or not even realize, that there is something off. I'm sure even the most emotionally healthy people will have one or two stories of wanting so badly to like someone that they tried (and failed) to make it work, but it just didn't.

The people in the first two categories seem like pretty good bets, although the first category, the so-called soulmates, might require some caution. It's sort of like the people with an innate talent in a sport or art form—it comes so easily at first that they don't have to do the hard work to be good. Eventually however, if they don't buckle down and work at it, they will plateau. If you have this deep, amazing soulmate-like connection with your partner, you may not notice (for a totally hypothetical example) that you have totally different goals in life, like that one of you wants to get married and travel while the other wants to join the army and kill people (again, totally hypothetical and in no way the exact thing that happened with one of my former paramours). Now, that doesn't mean that once you encounter those hurdles you can't then put in the work and figure out what to do next to continue your commitment to loving each other, but it does mean that you might get blindsided by them and that one or both of you may not actually be prepared to put effort in when it gets rough. (Hypothetically.)

I was lucky enough to have my first relationship ever be with someone who was, in most ways, totally wrong for me. Not only did we want different things out of life (I wanted to live in Vancouver, get married, and have babies and he wanted to live in Japan, probably not get married, and never have babies), but we were just mismatched. Among other differences, he is the type who needs a lot of space and alone time, while I needed the opposite of personal space and thrive in the company of others. Combined with the fact that we both had a lot of work to do in terms of recognizing our own self-worth and managing our own lives, and it was nearly impossible for us to meet our own needs, let alone be there for each other.

I say that this is lucky because I had a powerful lesson in how much it is not worth it to stick it out with someone who is wrong for you. There were good things about our time together, for sure, and I don't write off that whole relationship. New love is amazing and we were, at many times, enamoured with each other. It was also two years of regular loneliness, heartache, stress, and general bad feelings as I tried to figure out exactly why I was hurting so much while I was with someone who loved me. The fact that our relationship was at its best while he was on a long-term exchange to Japan says a lot.

So, have patience while you learn about yourself through your experiences with other people. Date them, try things out, but don't cling to someone who isn't the right one. It's really not worth it. It's also easier said than done. It takes a large dose of self-awareness to see when we are holding onto something that isn't working. I find it helps to try to think of it from an outside angle: if a friend told you all the things you feel in your relationship, how would you advise them? Alternatively, spend some quiet time with yourself. Breathe and ask yourself if you like this person and why. You may have to then practice honouring your worthiness, even if you don't really feel it's true yet. The act of standing up for yourself could even be a springboard to help push you towards valuing your true self even more.

Finding Love and Letting Go

So, if we were going to make a step-by-step list for finding love and partnership, what would that first step be? Here's what I can figure: it's being okay with the fact that you have relatively little control over meeting your life partner. Where and when you meet this sweet, sweet love is largely out of your hands.

You can literally meet "the one" (and by the one I mean that one person you will eventually end up committing yourself to, not your aforementioned non-existant one and only soulmate) anywhere and anytime. That means it could be next week, next year, or the next decade. Sound scary? It kind of is, but let's face it: you are awesome, and if it takes you 10 years to meet someone whose awesomeness compliments yours, it's well worth the wait. It helps if you can spend as much time as possible doing meaningful, fulfilling things in the meantime. Both you and the world will be much better off as a result.

Now might be a good time to address that whole notion that "once you stop looking for love and just do the things you enjoy, it will come to you." On one hand, that is complete bunk. People find love when they're looking for it all the time. If they didn't, then no one would meet their partner through online dating, set-ups, or when they go out to parties when they don't really feel like it but their friend said there would be other single people there. People like it because implies that everything is full of cause-and-effect relationships and that you just have to get to the right point in the story and you will live happily ever after. It also creates a handy culture of judgement over those who actively want love.

On the other hand, I think the reason this saying holds, aside from a huge confirmation bias where people look back on their lives and see it all as a story leading up to their current situation, is the fact that a lot of people meet someone in a particular moment or circumstance when they weren't expecting to meet anyone. For example, I have only met one partner in an environment where I specifically was looking to meet someone to date (we met online). The other times, they just popped up in life: one was a friend of my roommate and she had a party, another worked in my office for a year before I even considered him romantically, and the third I only met because a friend was going to a *Game of Thrones* screening and said she would buy me a drink if I came with her instead of going home.

I could say that I wasn't looking for love in those particular circumstances. I was, however, on the lookout for dudes in a more general sense, all those times.

More evidence that you have no idea where you'll meet someone: after going through what I like to refer to as Breakup 2.0: The Worst Breakup Ever, I started to identify very closely with every over-the-top metaphor about hearts ripping open and gaping voids left in souls. Heck, I even identified with Bella in *Twilight: New Moon*, which is really saying something irritating about how rough I was feeling, as she is one of the most annoying characters of all time in that book.

During that time a bunch of people were posting on Facebook about how it was their anniversary and how happy they were, saying things like "Four years ago today I met the man who is the father to my spawn and I couldn't be luckier!" Basically it was a "salt, meet wounds" sort of situation.

Then I realized something: these people were celebrating that they had met the love of their lives in some everyday, random environment. Whether it was at a party, work, class, or on the bus, the people I knew who had found love had found it in every conceivable life circumstance. You never know where this stuff is going to strike, and so you might as well try not to stress about it and pass the time doing things you enjoy.

Getting Out of There

Speaking of doing things you enjoy, here is the one thing that you do have control over! While you wait for the universe to align your path with that of some love-muffin, go out once in a while. While you don't know where or when you're going to meet that special someone, you do know it won't happen when you spend entire days in your living room marathon-watching *Angel* and reading web-comics.

If you are in a dark place and the thought of going out fills you with anxiety, fear, or just seems insurmountable, then I suggest practicing on a smaller scale. It's true that you aren't likely to meet someone to love in your living room with your door locked, but if "going out once in a while" feels impossible, then start with some loving kindness and baby steps. I strongly encourage you to work with a counsellor to help you through the process, because it is heavy lifting to relieve this burden all on your own.

Some things that have worked for me when I felt weighed down by the darkness:

1) Making small-scale social plans with friends who don't feel like work to be around;

2) Going for a short walk;

3) Taking my book or laptop to a coffee shop to work.

These worked for me because I tend to do better when I'm around people. Maybe you'll be more motivated to get out if you schedule a massage or go see a movie. Regardless, if just leaving the house feels like a major project to you, I encourage you to not worry about meeting a romantic partner at first, and focus on taking care of yourself.

Once you are out and about, I am not saying that you need to start trolling the town for unsuspecting kissing-partners every night, nor am I suggesting you start forcing yourself into some scene that isn't yours. All I'm saying is that you can increase your chances of meeting someone by actually leaving your home, ideally to places where you don't know everyone and may even spend time talking to some of those people.

This doesn't just apply to potential love-partners either! Meeting new people increases beauty, meaning, and connection in life in general! First of all, you're bound to learn something new. Secondly, you might be able to help that person in some way, which feels good. Third, you never know what this person could be to you: a friend, a love interest, the introducer of a love interest, your future new boss, or even the person who buys that old couch you've been trying to get rid of.

Life is full of possibilities, but you aren't going to experience any of them if you don't go out.

Now, some people just so happen to have a style of life where they meet new people regularly, be it through school, work, or that one friend who seems to know everyone and has a lot of parties. These are the people who seems to just turn around at the end of each relationship and have someone else waiting to love them. It won't even occur to these people to be concerned about where and when they will meet their next love interest, as it could be one of the many people they will meet in the next week, let alone the next 10 years.

Others have settled into their community of friends and family that might not change all that much for the next few years. If that's you, don't despair! First of all, be happy that you have such a strong foundation for your life and know who matters most to you. I am envious.

If you are, however, worried about finding new places to meet people, don't be afraid to take intentional steps to go out and try some new things.

Getting Online

Online dating: it's sort of like a big party where you have a friend whispering factoids about the other people in your ear and a shopping mall all mixed into one. Yes, it can be a dehumanizing mess of entitlement, but it can also be a very freeing space where you can, at the very least, be honest about what you're looking for and meet people you would never normally encounter in life. The key is to not take it too seriously.

This advice is especially true if you are having trouble seeing your innate value and the joy you could bring to someone else's life. The process can be daunting, from picking photos of yourself to writing a bio to the overwhelming feeling of putting yourself out there, hoping someone finds you appealing enough to talk to. It's vulnerable. Luckily, everyone you encounter online is in the exact same boat.

I know it's hip to be "so over" online dating and delete all the apps in favour of real life connections. That is fine if it's your preference, but there are a few benefits to online dating. For one, a person's basic stats are laid out in front of you, letting you skip the "How do I casually work this question into the conversation without being weird/superficial/prying?" dilemma.

Plus, if you're feeling melodramatically like there are no prospects for you in the world and you're just going to die alone, online dating shows you that there are actually a lot of other single people out there. Even if you're into something really specific, chances are there's an online dating community that reflects those interests.

If you're still unsure what you even have to offer someone in a relationship, it might be a good idea to go back to some earlier practices around cognitive-behavioural therapy and gratitude to help notice the things in yourself that add to the world. It could also be great to have a friend help, especially if you feel comfortable asking a friend of the gender or sex you are interested in dating.

Some things to watch out for in the online date-o-sphere: you will likely find yourself being way pickier than you would normally be. When all the facts are laid out in front of you without any of the actual warmth, charm, or personality of the human being that goes along with them, little things can easily become deal breakers as you swipe through potential dates. Try to check this behaviour in yourself, and remember this fact when you don't get responses from people you sent messages.

I tried online dating for the first time after my first relationship ended because I had never done that whole "casual dating" thing other people kept talking about. You know, where you get to know someone and whether you want a relationship with them *while* going on dates, not after you already know you are consumed by a burning, all-encompassing love for them. Since I've rarely experienced the phenomenon of being asked on dates in the real world, I figured that instead of waiting around for someone to ask me out, I would jump online. I learned that there are a lot of people out there who are looking for someone, and I experienced the joy of meeting a variety of people who I would have never encountered in my everyday life. It taught me to let rejections go, take my wins as they came, and gave me a little confidence that I had something to offer.

Rejection

A big part of dating is rejection. Objectively, it's really not that big of a deal. What are the chances that the next person you meet is going to be the "right one?" Pretty low! All rejection means is that both of you are getting closer to finding someone who is right for you.

It still sucks.

First of all, when you need to reject someone, it's really hard. You have to say something someone else won't want to hear, and, if you're a woman, you don't know if that person will get violent with you in response.

When I was in Grade 8 and getting ready for my first high school dance, my sister gave me some excellent advice: if someone asks you to dance and you don't want to, it's okay to say no. Seems obvious, but to a young girl with a penchant for letting herself feel uncomfortable to avoid making someone else feel bad, it was pure gold. Because of this helpful advice, I was able to actually say no when someone that I didn't know and felt uncomfortable with asked me to dance, saving myself from a potentially bad situation.

This sage advice from my sister carries over into so many areas of life! If you don't want to do something, be it dance with a person, date a person, kiss a person, or buy a potentially broken phone from a person on Craigslist, then just don't do it. You don't have to add anything to your life that you don't want to—especially broken phones.

It's also way more respectful to just be honest with someone. I don't know where in the evolution of dating etiquette everyone decided that just ignoring someone you aren't into is nicer than kindly telling them you are not interested, but I firmly disagree. All it takes is a simple "I enjoyed meeting you, but I don't feel a connection", or even just "No, thank you", and you've simultaneously acted with integrity and made that person's life easier.

Of course, that's just one form of rejection. What about when others are foolish enough to reject you? It always stings. Or burns. Or blows your heart out.

The only thing you can really do is remind yourself that if they're not that into you, then you don't want to be with them. What, are you going to convince someone to be attracted to you? Change their heart into one that "feels it" for you? In a mission to find a good partner, you're going to find a lot of mismatches along the way, so it only makes sense that you'll be a mismatch for someone else, too. It doesn't mean there's anything wrong with you, just that you weren't right for that person, and you're one step closer to finding the one you are right for.

This is cold comfort when there aren't any prospects on the horizon, especially if this was the first person of any potential to emerge in your path in ages, but nobody is your last chance. Yes, you may be older than you thought you would be. You may or may not have a biological clock ticking in your brain. You may not see how you will ever find someone else and the future may look like a big, empty desert. That is a really hard place to be. It's beyond frustrating to see a history of inability to find love and an empty future stretching out in front of you.

I get it. I've spent long stretches of time as a single person, and I have experienced the self-doubt, the millions of future-related questions, and the fear that it can entail. Through this process, I found that it was helpful for me to strive towards living a life that I want to hold onto regardless of finding someone and being open to change (because the one thing I do know is I am less likely to meet someone who just magically fits into my life exactly as it is; I've got to be flexible). It's a pretty fine line. Sometimes it will feel hopeless, and sometimes it will feel wonderful. Sometimes it will feel lonely, and sometimes it will feel like you have all the love you need. No need to pretend it's any different than it is. *Quirkyalone* by Sasha

Cagen is a slightly more light-hearted look at what it's like to be single in the long term.

This may be the most important thing I have learned in my time as both a single and coupled person: my quality of life and love consistently boils down to how much I value myself and my life, not my relationships. The more I have prioritized my own well-being and engaged in all my other practices to learn to appreciate myself, the more I have been able to be healthy and positive and find peace in the question and chaos of finding a mate.

As I write that, I have a little alarm bell ringing in my mind, because it sounds an awful lot like some of the philosophy I see in serene Instagram quotes: the "I can only follow my true path, and am not responsible for anything but my own happiness" philosophy. I am not a fan of a life that centres completely on oneself or disregards the impact you have on others. However, when your default is self-loathing, depression, anxiety, and low self-esteem, then it takes a hefty counterbalance of self-care and attention to turn around. We live in an interconnected world, and community, including loving romantic partnerships, cannot exist without a certain level of looking beyond our own needs. The foundation, though, has to be a firm awareness of our worth. When I believe I have value, that I am loved and that I deserve love (a belief I gained through the other practices outlined in this book), then I get to enjoy the foibles of romance for what they are, giving my heart to better people and sharing a healthier love.

Chapter 10: Feeling the Love

"Have you ever been in love? Horrible, isn't it? It makes you so vulnerable. It opens your chest and it opens up your heart and it means that someone can get inside you and mess you up." - Neil Gaiman

So, you've taken some risks, you've put yourself out there, and after fits and starts, some terrible dates and some decent ones that didn't call you back and maybe another dry spell where you wondered if you were going to find anyone ever again, here you are in a place where you maybe didn't expect to ever be: in a relationship, in love, or circling around a very strong mutual affection that seems like it could teeter into the love zone. Your former, single self may have been led to believe that once you reached this place of cute companionship, any insecurities you had would melt into nothing and your problems all fade away. Sorry, friend, but that's a big ol' lie. Some things might feel better—it's always nice to have someone there, and if the relationship is a good one, your partner is probably building you up and bringing out the better sides of your personality, which is bound to help you feel good.

You are still, however, you. You still possess all of your unique, magical qualities—as well as your insecurities and doubts. A relationship doesn't change that. And that's a good thing.

They say each relationship teaches us something. Here are a few of the somethings I have learned, and some of the differences I've seen in my relationships before and after learning to love myself.

About Them (or You)

Before I learned to value myself, the only place where I could experience validation was from my boyfriend. So I was incredibly needy and interpreted everything he did as a direct reflection of how he felt about me and my worth. It didn't help that he had his own issues that caused him to be kind of a master at pulling away and being unintentionally hurtful, but I wasn't able to interpret any of his actions with any perspective. Every disagreement, forgotten reply, argument, offhand comment, and difference of opinion was a knife to my non-existent self-esteem. I knew I couldn't expect him to read my mind, but I also kind of expected him to read my mind and just do what I wanted him to do to show he loved me. My logic said that if I wasn't happy it was probably his fault, because the whole point of having a partner is to be happy, right?

Now, thank goodness, things are different. Sure, I'll admit that I'm still a bit on the needier side when it comes to relationships. But now I can (usually) recognize when I'm being needy and see it for what it is. In part, this skill developed as a result of the counselling and self-work I had been doing around cognitive-behavioural therapy. By paying closer attention to the relationship between my thoughts and emotions, I was better able to notice my feelings and see how, while they are still valid, they are not necessarily the be-all-end-all. Feeling needy doesn't have to make me a terrible girlfriend. It means that I'm feeling a need, and if I can pay attention to it, I can try to meet it. Now, if I need something, I can try to take care of it myself or ask for it clearly and be appreciative when my partner responds by offering it instead of secretly resenting that he didn't think of it on his own. If I need to hear him say "I love you," I just ask him to. On the flip side, when I say "I love you" or do something kind, it's not an attempt to get him to say it back or teach him what he should be doing for me. It's simply an expression of love.

An important shift I have made over time is this: when I'm feeling generally unsatisfied with life or myself, I don't blame my partner. I (try to) take responsibility for my own feelings and life instead. This is because, unlike in the past, my entire life no longer revolves around them. When you make your life and self-worth all about your partner, then you make your happiness their responsibility, and it is relationship poison. I wasn't able to stop doing that until I learned to value my life for what it was while I was single. When I learned to shape my life into something closer to what I wanted it to be, it was easier to see that I was the architect of my own experience. I have learned that the quality of my relationship and the quality of my feelings about myself are two separate things. That makes a huge difference.

It's Not Worth it if it's Not Right

I've said this before, but, in my experience, it merits repeating: if your relationship isn't working, it isn't worth holding onto. This doesn't mean you never work in a relationship – maybe a lot. Work is, after all, what lifelong relationships are built on. But it does mean that, at some point, it might be better to walk away.

It can be easy to stay in something that's not working, whether it's to avoid feeling alone or because it feels safer to be in a less-than-good known entity than a big, dark unknown. It's also complicated by the fact that everyone is always saying that relationships are hard work. And it's true: relationships are hard work. So how do you know how much work is the right amount? Can it be too much? What percentage of the time should you feel like you're working really hard at it and not really happy or getting what you need? How much of it is about what you need versus what they need?

There's no definitive answer to those questions, and no numerical value to help make the choice clear. When I look back on the relationships where we were just wrong for each other and I was lying to myself about our future together, I can see the signs from very early on. I can remember the times I felt the niggling truth that I shouldn't be with them in the back of my head and ignored it. Those intuitions were all present very early on in those relationships, but the challenge lies in learning to recognize that voice earlier than later.

Like many things, learning to recognize and trust your intuition is an ongoing process, especially when your intuition may have previously been polluted by nasty beliefs that covered up your intrinsic value. My intuition, while perhaps trying to whisper truths to me all along, was drowned out, replaced, or impersonated very well with deep, dark beliefs that I didn't deserve anything good and might as well give in and die alone, so I couldn't have really trusted what I heard. As I learned to turn to, focus on, and believe the truth, however, I became better able to distinguish my inner voices.

I have experienced varying degrees of doubt in relationships. During my first relationship, I often felt deeply troubled by us as a couple. I was afraid to look at that troubled feeling because a part of me knew what the consequences would be, so I told myself that our love was enough and that we would have a beautiful life together. After our relationship ended, I told a friend, "Well, now I know what it's like to lie to myself about a relationship." And I did. I knew it well enough that, several years down the line I started a relationship with someone else where I intentionally looked at my feelings of doubt and said, "You're right, this won't work out, but, I am going to do this anyways and act as though it might." I was right. It didn't work out, and because love is as complicated as it is, I learned that knowing something isn't going to work out does not necessarily prevent you from getting your heart broken. Alas. At least I made a choice in the matter?

If you want to read up on recognizing warning signs in relationships, I recommend John Gottman. He was one of my favourite psychologists when I was in university, and he has developed an uncanny system of predicting relationship success as well as helping couples recognize their patterns and love each other better. His first book, *Why Marriages Succeed or Fail*, is a great introduction to the principles of his research, even if you're not thinking about getting married. His approach to relationships is very practical, while still embracing the more ephemeral elements of falling in love.

Keep Your Life

Fight the urge to ignore your friends and other obligations in the light of new infatuation! Everyone needs a different balance of time spent alone, with their partner, and doing their own thing with friends. Recognize what yours is, communicate, and maintain it. At the end of the day, you still need to be you. Even if you wind up spending the rest of your life with this person, you are still the person who spends the most time with yourself. Sacrificing who you are for someone else may have been your default when you did not see yourself as a wholly valuable person, but taking care of yourself is an important element in your ongoing cultivation of self-growth and self-worth.

Know How You Love

I'm big into the love languages. If you haven't heard of them, Dr. Gary Chapman writes about them in a book called *The Five Love Languages*. Dr. Chapman's main idea is that we all express and receive love in five primary ways: through gifts, words of affirmation, quality time, acts of service (doing practical things for each other), or touch. So, depending on who you are, you might be more inclined to express love—or wish to receive it—through a thoughtful gift, a deep conversation, taking out the trash, some sweet cuddles, or simply saying "I love you."

The concept of the book is that all five love languages are good things, and everyone appreciates them all to a degree, but there are one or two that will especially resonate with you. These are the ones that make you feel *especially* loved, and the ones you might require more than others. There are also some ways that you are more inclined to give love—these might be the same as how you receive it, but they might be different.

Knowing how you best give and receive love is incredibly valuable for a healthy relationship, as well as knowing how your partner gives and receives love. Maybe you're all about the quality time, but they like acts of service. So when they clean the kitchen floor, they feel like they've shown you how much they love you, and you're trying to tie them down for an involved date night, and both of you are feeling unappreciated and unloved.

Just because they receive love in a way that might not come naturally to you doesn't mean you're doomed—it just means you'll have to be intentional about showing it to them, as well as communicating your needs. You'll also then be able to better understand if they don't do something that makes you feel loved as often as you'd like—maybe it doesn't come naturally to them. This is where there is space to communicate your needs to each other. Perhaps you know that they are saying "I love you" by taking out the trash. By extension, they should be open to the fact that you are trying to express your love for them when you have to ask them to cuddle, again. These expressions of love might not be instinctual for either of you and moving towards a deeper understanding of what you and your partner need to feel loved will be key to better meeting each other's needs.

Know What You Want

Do you want a life that includes marriage and having children? Do you want casual fun? Do you want to find committed love outside of a written contract? Are you polyamorous?

You can't assume that anyone else wants the same thing that you want, so it's important to know what you're looking for. Depending on your age and life stage, this knowledge might not be a pressing, time-sensitive matter, but it's still helpful to know what you want your life to look like with when you find your partner of choice.

It's important to communicate those wants to the person you're with. It doesn't need to be communicated in a scary way: pressure-cooker questions like, "How soon are you going to propose?" can be intimidating for everyone, especially if they come up early in the relationship. But it's important to be honest about what your needs and wishes are and to be transparent about them with your partner. Conversations that begin with statements like, "This is what I'm looking for, and I'm interested to hear what you're looking for," can be clarifying. If you're anything like me, it will be a relief to know what your partner wants and how it connects with your vision for the future. If you have different long-term goals and decide to keep the relationship going, at least you've made an informed decision.

Know How You Need to Feel

Some books have terrible, cringe-worthy titles, yet they somehow manage to contain great advice. This is definitely the case for *How to Make Someone Fall in Love With You in 90 Minutes* by Nicholas Boothman. Worst title ever, right? But I appreciate his central claim, which is that you need to know who you are and what you need in order to find the right person.

One of his main points is that we don't necessarily fall in love with the person, but how we feel when we are with them. While (as usual) it's not that simple, I think he's on to something. After all, the reason I want to be with a guy who's taller than me isn't that I think short guys are unattractive, but because, as a tall woman, I feel less attractive and more ogre-like when I'm hovering over people.

Like all self-help writers, Boothman boils down our differences to a small number of key factors. In this case, he identifies four core feelings: he says that we all have a deep need to feel either important, powerful, intelligent, or special. Different people might bring out or undermine those feelings in us: a boss might always make you feel intelligent, or they may constantly make you feel like a fool.

When we find someone who brings out that core fe‹ desire, we are on our way to a good match.

Personally, I need to feel special when I'm in a relationship. If I feel like I'm special when I'm with you, I am over the moon. Others might love how being with their partner helps them feel like they could do anything or take on the world—that's a feeling of power.

If you want more detail on this, pick up the book. Feel free to download an e-copy so nobody sees the cover while you read it.

Communicate Everything

You may have noticed a trend throughout this chapter, and that's communication. Until we develop the actual ability to read minds, something I deeply hope never happens, communication will be the key to every relationship. If you don't communicate your needs, fears, wants, and desires, and don't listen while the other person is trying to communicate these things to you, then you can never truly know and be known by the other person.

When I was living under the weight of my self-hatred, communicating my needs was almost an impossible task. I didn't think I mattered at all, so why would my needs matter, to me or anyone else? I couldn't imagine anyone caring enough to want to hear or meet my needs, so what was the point? Besides, my needs were stupid and embarrassing. Conversely, when a need would grow to the point that I had to share it, I could not communicate in a loving, understanding, constructive way, because it was like a volcano of need bursting inside of me.

I see a direct relationship in my life between learning to see myself as a person with worth and my ability to communicate in a healthy, transparent, productive way. When I began to see myself as a person who deserved love, joy, peace, and meaning, I was better able to take charge of creating those elements in my own life. That included taking care of myself as well as recognizing when I had needed something from a partner. It also helped me have more empathy for other people who have their own needs, fears, and hopes and see that they are fighting their own battles in life.

All of these things helped me become a more conscious person and a better partner in relationships. And they all boil down to having a sense of self-worth. If you believe you are a creature of value, then you will see your own needs as worthy of attention—both your attention and your partner's.

Chapter 11: With a Heart that Breaks

"Stab the body and it heals, but injure the heart and the wound lasts a lifetime." -Minkeo Iwasaki

No matter how awesome you are, someone may one day drag your heart through the muck like nobody's business. That's because part of being awesome is being open and vulnerable with your heart and giving your love to someone—a risky endeavour.

The downside of loving fully is that it opens you up to a whole whack of heartache if that person, say, suddenly changes from a man into a scared little boy who can't commit to anything (after saying all sorts of commitment-like things) but is too cowardly to actually come out and say it so instead finds ways to manipulate you into breaking up with them and then, when you change your mind, get mad at you for loving them, all while slowly offering little pieces of information that they should have told you in the first place, parsed out over the course of months, thus stomping and grinding your heart into a little pulpy mess over and over again, because they couldn't do something like, oh I don't know, *tell* you up front that they've changed their mind and heart about everything to do with you, instead leaving the door open for you to keep offering them back a piece of your heart, only to have them slowly pick it into little pieces like a kid picks apart a leaf he absent-mindedly grabs off the nearest tree.

Oh, hey, did that get a little personal there for a second? Whatever, it's cool, I wasn't really that into him, I promise.

All of that is to say, sometimes your heart is going to feel like crap. What might make matters worse is that, if you've come around to see that you are worthy of love, you may be tempted to think "as a truly great person, I shouldn't be feeling this crappy, should I? I should know that I am okay and be able to shake this off like a slug off the bottom of my shoe."

I know I did.

Well, I am loathed to admit it, but as wonderful and worthy as we are, and as much as we may be growing in our awareness of this, we will feel truly, overwhelmingly awful sometimes. I also discuss this in the chapter on feeling feelings—bad feelings exist for a reason, and you can't, and shouldn't, make them go away. Getting mad at yourself for feeling bad will only make things worse. We have feelings. Yes, sometimes those feelings are made worse by terrible spirals of negative thoughts that we need to examine, question, and challenge. But they also sometimes happen because we have a loss in our lives, and that loss needs to be mourned. Ignoring your grief just means you have to spend more time dealing with those icky feelings later. We can't erase loss by pretending it didn't happen or that we don't care. Sometimes, the only way out is through.

Here are a few important lessons I've picked up by learning to value myself while also carrying a broken heart.

Don't Judge Yourself

Seriously, just don't. It doesn't matter if you think enough time has passed and you should be over it by now. It doesn't matter if the last time this happened it wasn't nearly this hard. It doesn't matter if no one else understands why you were so hung up in the first place or the relationship wasn't "long enough" to merit this kind of response. Recognize what you are feeling without judgment. Let it be there. Have compassion for your heart and make space for what it's feeling.

This is a great time to practice intentionally experiencing your emotions—something that is easier to do during heartbreak if you have already been working on it with less-extreme feelings. Instead of trying to shove them away, or unconsciously letting them swirl around you while you numb your brain with sugar, booze, and Netflix, try to enter into them. It's a matter of taking time to settle into your body and then identifying the core of how you're feeling and where you physically feel it in your body. Then you can observe it, hold it, and enter into it without it taking over your entire self. Because you're doing it with intention.

Head back to chapter four for a more detailed description of this practice, or, of course, read *Perfect Love, Imperfect Relationships* by John Welwood for a fantastically complete exploration. This book really breaks down this concept of moving into, and through, your emotions in a healthy, supported way.

Take Control of the Music

I mean that literally: try not to listen to sappy love songs or tragic heartbreaky music too much. Maybe you need a little bit of wallow time where you bond with Adele and feel like someone shares in your pain, but like attracts like and too much of it will only make you feel worse. The music we listen to makes a huge difference in how we feel. Unfortunately, this does mean that on top of the usual suspects (my heartbreak soundtrack consists of music by artists who lay their hearts bare with total honestly like Alanis Morisette, Adele, and Sarah McLachlan), other songs that were previously neutral or happy but now remind you of The One Who Shoved Miniature Exploding Bombs into Every Ventricle of Your Heart When You Weren't Looking might also become off limits.

It's tempting to convince yourself that one song *shouldn't* make you feel bad, and thus doesn't make you feel bad, but that falls more or less under judging and ignoring your feelings. Instead, if a song suddenly reminds you of your loss and makes you feel weepy, recognize it. Then try to be honest with yourself: is this really helping me right now?

Better than sobbing with Sarah McLachlan during my terrible heartbreak, I used music to help get through life. I made a playlist titled "Move On" that I listened to at least once a day. It was full of songs about awesome ladies doing awesome things for themselves and not needing men, as well as a few general party songs that made me feel happy and powerful. The idea wasn't necessarily to use the playlist as a weapon to banish the sadness, but to remind me of my capacity for strength, joy, and fun at least once a day.

For your reference and judgment, I present my playlist in its most recent incarnation (I still listen to it from time to time because it's just plain fun):

- Believe – Cher
- Eh Eh – Lady Gaga
- Ray of Light – Madonna
- Man Eater – Nelly Furtado
- Konichiwa Bitches – Robyn

- Gonna Get Along Without You Now – She & Him
- Daring Lousy Guy – Shivaree
- The Bitch of Living – Spring Awakening
- We Don't Want Your Body – Stars
- Tom's Diner – Suzanne Vega
- No Tonight (Ladies' Night) – TLC
- Creep – TLC
- Zero – Yeah Yeah Yeahs
- Bye Bye Bye – N'Sync
- Extraordinary Machine – Fiona Apple
- All is Full of Love- Bjork
- Shake it Off – Mariah Carey
- Kids in America – Kim Wilde
- No Scrubs – TLC
- Never Surrender – Corey Hart
- Big Wheel – Tori Amos
- I Do – Lisa Loeb
- Dance Dance Dance – Lykke Li
- I'm Good, I'm Gone – Lykke Li
- Dog Days Are Over – Florence + the Machine
- Stop Look & Listen – Belle and Sebastien
- Your Kisses Are Wasted On Me – The Pipettes
- You're So Vain – Carol King
- You Give Love a Bad Name – Bon Jovi
- Hold On – Wilson Phillips

Make your own list of songs that make you feel amazing and ready to put on your boots and walk all over anyone who gets in your way while busting a fabulous move. Listen to it. Repeat. If you start to associate one of the songs with too much heartache, knock it off the list. Listen to it again. Repeat.

If music isn't really your thing, then take some time to think about the TV shows, movies, podcasts, or books you take in. Are they comforting, or wallowing? Do they lift you up, or drag you down? Be intentional about your choices and set yourself up to experience joy at least once a day using whatever medium best suits you.

The Internet is for Masochism

If your former lover is in any way present on social media, avoid them at all costs. Hide them, mute them, unfollow them, or even block them if you must. It saves you so much heartache. Then do your absolute best to avoid intentionally visiting their pages. Chances are they are not posting updates about how miserable their lives are without you, so seeing them sharing about what they're doing in the glamorous, public face of their life won't make you feel better.

Get Out...

While there is a time and place for moping around the house, eating popcorn for dinner, and watching terrible TV, you can do that too much. Remember that whole chapter on doing things that make you feel great? Now, more than ever, is the time to try doing those things more often. Be easy on yourself, though. Don't flog yourself into doing something just to be miserable the whole time. What I'm going for here is more of an activity in which you find solace and rejuvenation, whether it's long walks with a good friend in nature, a massage, dance class, or a spiritual activity that nourishes you. Don't feel forced to whip yourself into a fury of activity; the goal is to gently re-integrate pleasurable activities into your life at a time when doing so may feel counterintuitive.

...With Other People

Being alone from time to time is an important part of personal growth and mending a broken heart. Alone time is when you can reflect on who you are and what you want and can involve journal writing, meditation, or going for a meandering walk. There are also times, however, when seeing a good friend can truly nourish your soul. Tread gently and practice some extra kindness to yourself when making choices about who you're choosing to spend time with when you are feeling more vulnerable than usual. Consider a friend or family member who feeds your spirit—not all of our friends and family are consistently there for us, and now is an especially important time to draw boundaries around who you're spending time with, and how. For example, you might not want to be with the friend who just started dating someone new and is head over heels about them when your own heart is mush, or it might feel particularly arduous for you to spend a long evening with a friend for whom you find yourself shouldering the burden of emotional labour on good days. Pick the one who's fun and listens to you while reframing things in a helpful light.

In general, the people we surround ourselves with have a huge impact on our outlook and well-being, and this impact multiplies when we are vulnerable. This doesn't mean you should only ever hang out with people who agree with you or are a good time, all the time, but it does mean that when your heart is hurting, you have full permission to be cautious about who you spend time with. A good hint as to whether someone will be helpful or hurtful to be with during fragile times is simply to pay attention to your instinctive reaction to being with them. If they invite you to hang out, or you even just think about being with them, and feel your stomach drop, your shoulders tighten, or you feel that you are suddenly on high alert, perhaps they are not the first person to be with right now.

Those Dang Thoughts

No matter whose idea it was to end the relationship, as you move into a new reality of life without your former partner, you may find yourself replaying key conversations and things you wish you had said to them in your mind. If you're anything like me, you won't even know you're doing it until you realize that you are mime-acting-out what you wish you had told them while waiting for the bus. In a crowd. It's cool. Remember the very first step? Don't judge it! Just try to stop. First of all, as much as I'm in favour of challenging social boundaries, watching someone have a one-sided mime-argument is probably more creepy than sociable for everyone else. Secondly, these are not helpful thoughts. Enlist your Inner Thought Vigilante and bring back those mad cognitive behavioural skills, switching those thoughts over to something else.

Remember the key and subtle difference between turning off these repetitive, unhelpful thoughts and avoiding necessary feelings. Feelings of loss and sadness are a natural part of losing someone. Feelings of anger are a natural part of being hurt. Reviewing conversations over and over in your mind, however, leads to nothing but reliving old hurts, or creating new, imagined ones, and that is neither necessary nor helpful. Thinking about how you are pathetic and unloveable attacks your core self and is a harmful lie.

If you find yourself in a situation where you need to turn your thoughts around, you might have a hard time thinking of something to distract yourself. All those poopy thoughts will cloud anything positive. This could be a good time to distract yourself with your Good Times playlist, or to start listing everything your grateful for, from the fact that you have legs that can walk to the fact that your head is still attached to your body. You can even prepare in advance by storing up mental or physical lists of things that are good in your life: people who make you laugh, favourite TV moments, that time you got an Emmy award (hey, people who win Emmy Awards get their hearts broken too), whatever. Turn your thoughts around to these more positive endeavours, even if it's only to take a brief reprieve from the spiralling conversations going through your head. Reprieves are good. Each little moment of reprieve reminds your heart that there is more to you than the pain you are currently feeling, until eventually, you are standing on more hope than pain.

Batten Down the Hatches

You know how in movies and TV shows, people who are heartbroken walk in a slump down the street and break out into comical tears every ten steps because they see the restaurant, the bus stop, or the shop where they used to spend time with their beau? You know how it's painted as comically pathetic and ridiculous? Sadly, as anyone who's had their heart clawed out knows, it's also real.

I was shocked and horrified at how many reminders of my heartbreaker I found around me, and how much they affected me. The restaurants we went to, the places we strolled hand-in-hand whilst joyfully discussing our future dream home, the store where I bought him a birthday present, and cars that look just like his were everywhere. I would be riding the bus when all of a sudden, *bam!* One of these landmarks would punch me in the face and I would be fighting back tears that didn't feel very comical at all.

That's not even accounting for the non-physical landmarks: the date that would have been our anniversary; the annual event that had been our "coming out party" as a couple; the date on the calendar when I assumed we would have gotten back together, even though we were breaking up—those emotional landmarks were even worse than the physical ones. While the restaurants and cars would jump up out of nowhere, hitting me with random pain that would eventually subside, these dates and events were visible from a distance. I had weeks—months, even—to feel their impending doom and practice my preparatory suffering. It was... unpleasant.

There's no way that I have found to really deal with this except to let it come. Quickly shove sunglasses on your face if you're alone in public and don't feel like broadcasting your tears. Take deep breaths. Recognize the loss and whatever feelings are accompanying it. Reach out, if you are in a position to do so and be honest about what you are feeling. Know that this random pain isn't all that's left of you.

As far as I know, there is no miracle cure for true heartbreak. If you never really cared for the other person, that's one thing. When the rug of love has been pulled out from under you and then used to knock you over every time you try to stand up, however, it's a whole different ball game, and it sucks. It will suck a lot, and then, in a process that takes more time than you would like, it will suck less and less. Just remember, don't judge yourself. Let your heartbreak take the time it needs.

As an aside, I recommend putting in some extra effort to look super fine during this time, because that can sometimes help. At the very least, a) if you run into the offending party you'll look great; b) getting checked out by others is a bit of a confidence booster (even if you don't see it happening, you can imagine heads turning while you walk down the street); and c) when you catch your reflection in a car window you'll get an instant boost instead of a little kick lower at how you look as sad as you feel.

Don't Make Excuses for Them

Actions speak louder than the stories you're making up in your head.

If you truly, honestly love and trust someone, you will probably justify some (or all) of their bad behaviour. That's just part of what we do in life for the people we love. A friend is late, for example, not because they are inconsiderate but because they are super busy and doing their best. In a relationship, however, we can take this a step too far by telling ourselves that, for another totally hypothetical example, the person we love really does love us back, but is freaked out because they lost a job, and once they have some time to cool off they'll come crawling back to us with a grand gesture—something simple, like when Heath Ledger performs a ridiculous rendition of "Can't Take My Eyes Off of You" in the movie *Ten Things I Hate About You*—and everything will be perfect again. Sure, they're pushing you away now, but it really is just because of the job they lost, and that's it.

Guess what? If they are pushing you away, then *they are pushing you away*. End of story. That is the very unsatisfying end to this story, but that's okay because life is not a story. People change, they hurt you, they leave issues unresolved, and they fail to see the error of their ways (no matter how romantic of a turnaround it would be if they did). If they were to change their ways, that's great, but you can't sit around waiting for it. Holding onto the possibility that they actually still want you makes it impossible to forgive and move on.

In fact, recognizing someone's behaviour and walking away is one of the healthiest things you can do.

As my dad said while I was going through the many stages of heartache of my worst break-up, "Guys are not complicated."

Normally I bristle at statements like this because they boil an entire group of people down to a single trait, which seems unfair. However, the more I look at the world, the more I think that (in general, allowing for exceptions), guys are, indeed, not very complicated. Neither, really, are women. People may seem complicated, but when it comes to this kind of stuff, we're all pretty straightforward. At the end of the day, the extraneous explanations we make up in our heads to explain why someone is treating us terribly don't really matter. What matter are the offending (or non-offending) party's actual actions. At some point, it is useful to ask yourself what is the simplest explanation for these actions? If the simplest explanation is that they are acting out of love for you, then great! If not, then you've got a problem on your hands, and you need to treat it accordingly.

Not to say that you just walk away when someone does something inconsiderate, of course. By all means, bring it up, talk about it, communicate, and do all that good relationship stuff. There is, eventually, a time and a place for letting go—maybe because they are actively pushing you away or because you realize they're not even trying to hold on.

Actions speak louder than the stories you make up in your head. You deserve better than stringing yourself along because you see the potential for change.

Avoid Revenge

I never understood the whole psycho ex-girlfriend thing until I had my heart really and truly broken. All of a sudden I experienced a deep, vindictive need for revenge that I had never before felt in my life. My thoughts would whirl with questions about the tools at my disposal to hurt him the most: names I could call him, people I could date, things I could do to his home or car. While I knew that he was dealing with some big, difficult things and that he was experiencing some pain, there was no way he was feeling enough pain and sorrow for what he had done to me, and I wanted to suffer like I was suffering.

Luckily, I managed to hold myself back, and I think the worst I ever did was send an email with some less-than-well-thought-out phrases. I call this lucky for a few reasons: first of all, devoting your actions to hurting someone else is not a recipe for healing, ever. Second, even if it was, it's pointless. If another person has stopped loving you, you can never really get the revenge you seek, because nothing you do will hurt them in the way they hurt you. It's a truly painful thing to come to terms with: they no longer care in the same way you care, which means that any act of revenge on your part is really just kind of sad.

Forgiveness is hard, especially if a person never actually apologizes. In fact, one of the best definitions of forgiveness I've heard is that it is accepting the apology you never received. For me, forgiveness is ongoing and comes in phases. The first phase is intellectual forgiveness, where I decide to forgive them. In most ways, this decision is driven by my exhaustion. Holding on to anger and judgment is tiring, and it hurts. Not as much as the heartbreak, perhaps, but it still hurts. After a while, it's too much, and I have to let it go. A part of intellectual forgiveness, for me, is to intentionally think with compassion about them and whatever pain in their life brought them to where they are now.

Then comes a slower process of emotional forgiveness. For me, that comes in the form of a daily practice of choosing to look at the person with compassion. I remind myself that, like all of us, they are a hurt person trying to make their way through life and making mistakes on the way. So, when my own hurt and anger wells up, it becomes a practice of feeling what's there without needing to place blame for it—and, importantly, without needing to demonize its source.

Over time, with a lot of ups, downs, and inner rage-monologues that make me wonder if I have made any progress at all, that practice of emotional forgiveness loses its utility as a daily ritual. My thoughts about this person become less frequent. Perhaps they come up once a week, or once a month, when previously they happened daily. Then, eventually, I realize I haven't thought about them for ages, and when I do, I don't want them to hurt anymore. Maybe I even, actually, want the best for them.

While there isn't always an endpoint to forgiveness where we can confidently say we've "moved on" and be left without any complicated feelings, I think that the ability to truly wish the best for someone who hurt you is the ultimate form forgiveness can take. I have a lot of trouble letting go of my hurts, so I need to do it through an intentional practice. Whether you find my method useful or would rather seek your own path to forgiveness, moving from raw hurt, anger, and vulnerability to compassion and hope for the future will set your heart free.

Chapter 12: Back Off, Barnacles

"Have no fear of perfection—you'll never reach it."

- Salvador Dali

Once you begin to see your value more clearly and find that your-self actually believing that you have worth, it may feel safe for you to begin to examine the parts of yourself that you have trouble making peace with. The things that, perhaps, you don't like about yourself and that cling to you like a barnacle sticks to a rock: they are hard, pointy, and uncomfortable, but they don't feel like they are integral to who you really are. They could be scrubbed off if you really wanted to put the work in.

For a few examples: I never take out the garbage; I am often em-barrassingly loud; I over share things other people might consider "personal" or "uncomfortable" or "inappropriate" quickly, easily, and in public with my too-loud voice; because I love research, I can easily come across as a know-it-all; I can get a little too into gossip. Of course, those are just the things I'll admit to myself—the barna-cles I can see. Find one of the people in this world who don't like me, or one of my siblings, and they'll probably have truly annoying things to share about me.

They are also all things that I could work on changing if I really wanted to. I could start trying to get into the habit of taking out the garbage or pay closer attention to how I share the cool new study I read about and whether I am actually just showing off my knowl-edge.

I used to spend a lot of time thinking about these aspects of my personality that I consider negative. I would spend entire evenings going over in my head stupid things I had done or said, staring at and analyzing my barnacles. These cycles would reinforce what I eventually came to misperceive as facts: that with all these annoying habits, none of my friends must actually like me. It was a very dark, lonely time. Every phone call, every hug, and every kind word went through the filter of my self-loathing and entered my heart as a lie.

Today, things are different. I no longer spend the majority of my waking hours thinking about my barnacles. Sometimes those less-than-awesome thoughts bubble up (because, as Lucas says in the 90's teen classic *Empire Records*, "Who knows where thoughts come from? They just appear!"), but I no longer dwell on them with the same frequency as I used to. Over time and through the techniques laid out at the beginning of this book, especially the cognitive behavioural work and gratitude practices, I have become better at identifying these thoughts as simply thoughts, and letting them go, while still recognizing that there may be some things—barnacles—that I would like to change about how I operate in life.

A Simple Solution

So you've figured out something about yourself that you don't like. You're taking a cue from Michael Jackson and starting with the (wo)man in the mirror. Before you try to take further steps to work through it, let's check in to make sure it is, indeed, in the realm of changeable behaviours and, vitally, not based on a negative lie about your worth as a person. When facing a piece of yourself that you don't like or want to change, ask yourself these questions:

1) Is it an overarching statement of general terribleness?

2) Does it involve you reading other peoples' minds of what they must be thinking about you?

3) Is it inherently unchangeable?

4) Is it a specific thing that is based on behaviour instead of who you are as a person, and that you feel is legitimately getting in the way of your relationships/job/happiness/life?

Just like all magazine quizzes, the correct answers were probably a dead giveaway: your first three answers should be "no" and your last one a "yes." The first three point to problems that are either imagined or unactionable and are likely rooted in a deeper issue of not yet believing in your inherent worth as a person. These kinds of beliefs need to be confronted and dealt with on a deeper level, as outlined in the first few chapters. The last question, on the other hand, identifies a barnacle: it's not a deep part of who you are, and it's something you can actually work on and change.

Get ready for this, because my big solution is going to sound a lot like the solution in the chapter about doing things you like: 1) think of the thing you don't want to do; then 2) stop doing it.

Easy, right?

Wait.

It's not that easy, is it?

The real challenge here is overcoming our habits and go-to reactions. Not that these can't be powerful things, but at the end of the day this is only behaviour we're talking about, not some integral part of who you are. You are not your bad habits. Interrupting coworkers, jaywalking, talking too loud, a lack of discipline, or compulsive shopping habit are external traits that can be changed. Barnacles can be annoyingly difficult to get rid of, but they aren't actually a part of the rock they cling to, after all.

The Steps

So, let's get practical. Take the thing you don't want to do anymore, like gossiping. I kind of love gossiping, Not in the "spreading lies about other people" sense, or even the "sharing secrets that were confided to me in confidence" sense, but more in the "knowing everything that's going on in other peoples' lives and talking about it" sense. It's probably not the best habit because most of those things I love to gossip about are probably none of my business, and while I'd never share something that a person shared with me with the expectation of secrecy, I do enjoy divulging scandalous things I've heard through the grapevine. So, I'm trying to stop myself from gossiping because I feel like it's getting in the way of the kind of person I am deep down inside.

First things first: prepare for battle. Much like those destructive thought patterns we talked about, right now gossiping, for me, is an instinctive habit. I've done it so many times that I don't even realize I'm doing it until it's too late. So the first thing I'm going to do is think about situations where this is more likely to come up and friends that bring out my gossipy nature. This anticipation helps remove the element of surprise that gossiping has over me.

I also need to understand that I gossip for a reason. It makes me feel like I'm in the loop, included, and involved in peoples' lives. It's fun. I might even feel a little bit important if I know something someone else doesn't. These emotions are a powerful draw for me. My deepest insecurities come from feelings of exclusion, of being left behind and forgotten. (Hello, I'm a middle child, how are you?) So I need to be aware that I might feel kind of crappy and left out if I disengage from gossip, but also remind myself that those feelings will be temporary and that it's not gossiping that keeps me involved in other peoples' lives but being caring, fun, and respectful of everyone's boundaries.

Ask yourself: what emotional response does your barnacle give you? What need does it fill?

This could wind up touching on some very deep nerves and if you find yourself reacting strongly to it, you know you're onto something. It also could mean that you need to talk to someone about it. That could be a wise and caring friend, or it could be a counsellor, depending on how deep that nerve goes and how serious you are about dealing with it. It can feel easier to just give up and ignore it, or to walk with a swagger and say things like, "If you can't take me at my worst you don't deserve me at my best!"

But if it's really getting in the way of your life or the person who you want to be, it's worth working on.

The next step is to act like Mad-Eye Moody (that's a *Harry Potter* reference, for you non-geeks out there) and act with constant vigilance. I already have an idea of where I'm going to encounter my nemesis gossip, usually when I am hanging out with a group of witty girlfriends who I want to "keep up" with, and the emotional hold it has on me. Now I just need to watch out for it.

Chances are good that at first (even with all that prep work) I usually won't realize what's going on until it's too late. I will find myself mid-gossip and be horrified by the person I continue to be. It's okay. Habits are tough to break, and melodramatic hyperbole about being a horrible person may be funny but is not actually helpful.

Perhaps more helpful is a yoga-inspired practice of observing that you have strayed, and bringing yourself back onto your path. So, even if it might be embarrassing (and let's be honest, a little embarrassment will probably help me remember to avoid gossiping in the future), every time I catch myself gossiping I'll stop myself mid-track, say something like "Sorry, I just realized I'm gossiping and I'm trying to stop," and then change the topic. Socially awkward, but effective.

This phase of constant vigilance lasts as long as it takes to stop myself from gossiping before I start.

Depending on what your barnacle is, you might also want to consider making your quest to remove it public. That way your more helpful friends might help you realize that you're doing it or might avoid enabling the behaviour.

There are experts like Jeremy Dean, author of *Making Habits, Breaking Habits*, who say that it takes anywhere between four to eight weeks to make something a habit, and the same goes for getting rid of a habit. So set a concrete goal and go for it. Just think of how awesome you feel when you successfully stop doing something that annoys you. And if it takes a while, that's cool too. Habits are not made or broken all at once, but in little bits here and there.

The Perspective

I'd like to tag on some extra emphasis to the fact that we have bad habits for a reason. As I mentioned, my compulsion to gossip is connected to my desire to feel included, because I have major insecurities around feeling left out. When I'm out of the loop on what's happening in peoples' lives, my gut reaction is to believe they don't care about me.

In fact, it seems to me that a lot of our darker sides have to do with either getting or deflecting attention because at some point in our lives we learned that in order to feel safe and loved we needed either to make everyone look at us or make them look at someone else. We either needed all the attention to feel loved, or the attention terrified us and made us feel unsafe. People needed to prove that they loved us by fulfilling certain criteria, and if they didn't, we knew to barricade our hearts against them.

Sure, some bad habits are just bad habits; I never take out the garbage because it's the last thing on my mind and it feels like a lot of work to walk outside in the rain, but it's not rooted in a deeper fear of exclusion, failure, or a core wound that I've carried from childhood. Many of the things we do that we want to stop and change about ourselves, however, exist for a reason. In my experience, ignoring the reason just makes it stronger and just creates more anxiety and pressure around the change.

Chapter 13: We've Got Soul

"We are so ruined, so loved, and in charge of so little." -
Anne Lamott

I believe we all have souls. I don't know what they look like or what it means exactly. I don't think it's a physical thing inside of us or remotely measurable. I just have a deep sense that there is something about us, within us, connecting us. And it's bigger than us.

To be a little less vague for a moment, let's talk science. So far psychologists, neurologists, and psychiatrists have been unable to define or explain where our sense of self lives in us. Not the individual behaviours and chemical reaction, but our overall consciousness, our ability to mindfully monitor our thoughts, feelings, and behaviours and put them together as a cohesive "I." There are some competing theories out there, but as far as I've been able to find in my reading, no one has put their thumb on it quite yet. I think that this consciousness is part of what I'm referring to when I say that we humans have souls. (Also, I don't necessarily think souls are limited to humans, I just have no experience being an animal or a tree, so I won't speak for them.)

I also mean that we are connected: to something greater, something eternal, or something that unifies us all as creatures under the sun. I'm sure a part of this can be explained by some advanced physics and cognitive psychology, although to be honest, I don't really care. What matters to me more is the fact that I can feel this connectedness and that it creates meaning for me.

Ultimately, I am saying that human beings are more than just bones and meat and arrangements of molecules, and, to take it a step further, that ignoring this side to our being cuts us off from a huge amount of humanity and connection – that which makes us into creatures of awe.

I'm not going to tell you how you should pursue a better relationship with your soul, if you want to join me in believing that you have one. In my yoga teacher training, I was introduced to a concept regarding all myths, religions, and spiritual practices: they are all maps, and they are all maps of the same territory, each showing different qualities. Sort of like how you can have a map of a city that includes the roads, another that shows bike paths, and another that shows all the pipes, electrical lines, and sewers. They all cover the same ground, and they all reveal something that is valuable—depending on what you need.

Personally, the map I connect with most is the Christian map. Perhaps it's because that's how I was raised, perhaps it's because it's a story of a God who, as I read it, tries to meet us where we are at instead of requiring us to change for him, and that speaks to me.

Of course, I grew up with the Christian story as the dominant story in my life, but I haven't followed it my entire life. I went through a fairly long stretch of ignoring God, church, and everything connected to it. I thought, and still think, that it is truly possible that everything to do with God and religion is an invented reality that we have come up with in order to feel like our lives have meaning. Living in an indifferent and accidental universe where horrible things happen that we don't understand is scary, so why wouldn't the earliest humans start inventing gods to explain things and give us meaning, as well as social cohesion?

On the flip side, it could be real. We could have an innate yearning for the eternal, great spirit that connects us all because there is one.

Either way, we will never really know. God, if he (they? She?) is real in any form, is on the other side of a great unknown that humanity will never, ever be able to nail down. There are scientists who have tried to disprove God. They can't. We also can't prove he (it?) is real. No attempt to use science or logic can give a definitive answer one way or the other, because God and our spiritual selves are not a part of the same world as logic and aren't interested in the same questions.

One day I made a connection I hadn't made before: I have a choice. It's a matter of perspective. I have, for example, chosen to take an optimistic perspective on life, not because the beautiful, exquisite, wonderful parts of life are more real than the cruel, empty, horrible parts, but because life is better when I look for the good first. As the Dalai Lama says, "Choose to be optimistic. It feels better."

So is life better, for me, when it is connected to a God who loves me and wants to be in a relationship with me. I'd rather live a life where everything has meaning than where everything is random.

What about you? What does your soul—the unexplainable part of you that holds all your experiences, longings, and gives you a sense of connection and meaning—pull towards? Is there a myth, or a map, that grabs you?

If we get functional for a minute, connecting to a spiritual practice that has meaning for you has other practical benefits.

Spirituality with Benefits: Self-Worth

One of the main benefits, I have realized, of embracing the concept of a God who loves me as an individual is that it means I must be worth something as an individual human. How can I be worthless when I am loved and accepted exactly as I am? When I was, actually, made to be this exact person? With God, I am enough. I am acceptable and accepted. I am loved. I screw up and do crappy things, but that doesn't change the core of acceptance around me.

In fact, since I believe God loves every single person (yes, including Hitler), as well as the rest of creation, it puts a perspective and reverence around everything and everyone. It helps me when I'm struggling to forgive people who hurt me, to remember that they are loved for who they are, too. It helps me to respect nature to remember that it is a beloved creation. It helps me to value the lives and treatment of animals. (Not that I need a God-figure to respect people, nature, or animals without a sense of greater connection, but it sure becomes more salient when considered in the light of creation.)

Spirituality with Benefits: Community

Joining a spiritual community or church is really an instant community. I mean, the other members are humans like any other, so it can be a bit of work to make break in, but once you do it, you have connected to a group of people who are interested in living life in a better way, and doing it together: people who are open to hearing about your struggles and triumphs, and mourning or celebrating with you; people who tend to be fairly generous with their abilities and time, in the service of others; people who want to make the world a better place. Find one that fits and challenges you, and you have found something worth holding on to. Plus, feeling connected to a community is one of the number-one predictors of having a longer, healthier, happier life.

Spirituality with Benefits: Prayer

Then there's prayer. I spent a lot of time feeling like I was wasting time talking at walls with prayer. Then I realized a few key things.

One: when I pray about something, I am forced to be completely honest about it. Or, at least, it's harder to lie to myself. God already knows everything, so there's no point in lying to him, after all. I can reveal and examine the true desires of my heart, the ones that I might not really admit out loud. I can discuss something that I feel like I should have let go of ages ago. I can be real.

Two: there is a sense of giving it up. I have been greatly comforted by the idea of laying my worries at God's feet. It's different than asking God to do things and praying for outcomes. Praying for outcomes feels like a rather selfish way of approaching God. It's transactional and, if you think about it, doesn't really make sense. If I'm asking for something that benefits me, chances are that someone else in the world would benefit from the opposite. Why on earth should I get a sunny day for my birthday when a farmer desperately needs rain for her crops? This attitude seems counter to the point of simply connecting to the source of my life.

Instead, I've begun approaching prayer with the attitude that I will hand things over: my stresses, worries, fears, and pains—both for myself and others— and trust that The One Who Knows Me Way Better Than I Know Myself will take care of things.

This doesn't mean inaction on my part. I am not into sitting back and waiting for God (or the universe) provide for everything. It's more about sharing of the load, and boy is it a relief.

Three: it gives me a valid excuse to share my struggles with people who care. It can be hard to just up and tell someone you're struggling with, afraid of, or worried about something. In a spiritual community, however, prayer is a totally acceptable reason to share anything. Ask for prayer while you navigate through a new job, a sick family member, challenging relationship, anything. The result is people who know you, hear your struggles, and care about them. The fact that they pray for you may or may not practically result in anything, but it draws community closer, reminds you that you're not alone, and if it inspires actual change, well that's a wonderful bonus.

Looking Outside Ourselves

Many people see religious morality as all framed around the afterlife: be good now so that you get a great reward in the great beyond. Personally, I don't connect with this idea. Nobody really knows what's going to happen after we die, and if you're only doing good so that you don't get in trouble later, I'm not sure that's really all that good in the first place. My spiritual practice is about living life with meaning now and connecting to something bigger than me, as well as reminding me that life is not all about me. It gets me looking outside myself and into something greater.

I think we humans were meant to live for something that is not ourselves. That's one of the reasons why so many of us want to be paired off in relationships and ultimately procreate. Sure, there's the whole survival of the species argument, and it's a good one, but I think there's more to it. When you partner with someone for life, and even more so when you have a child, your life is no longer just about you. Part of loving someone is considering them and their needs before your own once in a while. It's desiring their happiness and well-being, dedicating your joys and successes to them as well as mourning losses together.

How many people work boring jobs for the good of their families? Sacrifice time, resources, and in-the-moment happiness to support their spouses? Sit through terrible, awful plays because their daughter will walk across the stage and say one line? These are not rational actions if we are living only for ourselves.

We do the same things for the other people we love—our friends and parents. Heck, we sacrifice money and time regularly for the sake of our pets. And if it isn't a relationship, chances are we're still living for something else—a job, perhaps. Status and wealth. National pride.

Basically, what I'm saying is that we are all dedicating our lives to something, and it may not be what we think—or would like. Think about what you take most seriously, what you sacrifice the most for, and peel back the layers of what is really behind it. It may have to do with connecting with community. It may have to do with connecting with your soul and your spirituality. It may also have to do with reputation, ego, or wealth.

Whenever I have a strong, instant, negative emotional reaction to something, I try to look at what's underneath. What am I trying to protect, preserve, or promote? At the end of the day, it is often me and my image. For me, that's not good enough. I don't want my life to boil down to me. I want it to be about something bigger. (I realize this may make me sound a lot more in control of my life and my responses to it than I really am. Please note the "try" in that first sentence! I am not a superior being who always recognizes their true intentions and I have a ton of blind spots.)

Just deciding to make your life about something bigger isn't enough, though. Like everything in this book, it takes practice. It takes conscious effort and intention. You've got to decide what you want your life to be about and then work on some self-awareness to see when you're actually feeding that thing.

Whether you want to join an established religion, start meditating, study a variety of scriptures, jump into yoga, or enjoy the wonder of nature through scientific exploration, there are many ways for you to connect with your soul. If this soul stuff sounds weird, think of it as an experiment. Ask yourself, "If I did have a soul, what would feed it?" Then try doing that thing with a full and open heart and see what happens. You may find a greater source of strength, power, and awe.

Chapter 14: With a Heart Unbuttoned

"Because true belonging only happens when we present our authentic, imperfect selves to the world, our sense of belonging can never be greater than our level of self-acceptance." - Brené Brown

Learning how to be vulnerable has been a scary but vital part of my journey towards wellness and loving myself. At the outset, I didn't feel a strong connection to this idea. Sure, vulnerability is important to relationships, but why would my ability to be vulnerable have any connection to feeling good about myself?

After all, I felt like I was already really vulnerable. I'm the kind of person who will easily share things that other people might difficult to share—stories where I look totally foolish, feature terrible relationship events, or about my struggles with depression. But it wasn't until one of my friends made an offhand comment that I was a closed book that I began to reassess myself. I thought I was an open book: ask me anything about myself, after all, and I'll tell you. As it turns out, that's not entirely what vulnerability is. Vulnerability is about sharing the things that are hard to share, whatever those things are for you. It sounds obvious, but I needed it pointed out to me, first by my counsellor, and then through the writing of people like Brené Brown. In her book *Daring Greatly* she goes into detail about what it means to be truly vulnerable. If it's easy to share, it isn't truly vulnerable, and it isn't really letting people in, at least not into that inner sanctum of your heart where your deepest hopes, fears, and your need to be known reside.

Personally, I am generally fine with sharing anything under two conditions: first, it's important to me that the person I'm sharing with asked, so I know that they care and want to know, and secondly, I feel comfortable sharing if what I'm sharing is coming from a place where I feel confident in the moment. I can tell people how yesterday I was feeling really crappy and cried for no reason if today I'm fine and have a running theory on what was upsetting me. I can tell people about the terrible crushing my heart received several years ago if I don't have to admit the times that it suddenly gets raw again and I don't know why.

But here's where my real vulnerability lies: I hate admitting to anything to do with loneliness or wanting to find love. I hate even typing it. As a youngish, independent, city-living gal, I feel like I'm somehow failing at feminism if I admit that all I really want is to have someone to come home to and raise some babies with (while still doing a whole bunch of other stuff at the same time). That's vulnerable because that's what I don't want people to see when they look at me.

So why can't we just hide those parts of ourselves away? If we don't want anyone to see them, why don't we just keep them secret? Won't everything will be fine, then?

How Vulnerability Helps You

Vulnerability is good for us, as terrifying as it is, because we are all relational creatures. Humans need each other, and we need to feel loved and accepted by each other. Most of our shouting, angry, dark voices have some root in that need, and many of our worst traits are cover-ups or compensations for our fragile inner Bambi who hasn't found his Thumper yet. But here's the thing: we can't find love and acceptance—and, importantly, forge the kind of bonds that challenge the darkness—if we don't let people see our darkness.

True love (and here I'm referring to a more universal type of love, not romantic love) is born when people share deep truths about themselves and then stick around, doing the hard work of continuing to love each other when they've seen the full range of who their loved one truly is. True love is sticking around so you and your loved one can ugly cry, scream, or haltingly confess dark secrets together. And it doesn't have to be all doom and gloom and five-hour heart-to-hearts; that would be exhausting. True love also involves a good dose of fun. But if nobody gets access to these vulnerable parts of who you are, you may never really know whether they love you or the version of you that gets polished up for public viewing.

I can tell you that letting people see my dark, snotty, pathetic, whiny, needy side is one of the scariest things in the world, and that when they stick around afterwards, I feel exponentially more loved by them and connected to them.

How Vulnerability Helps Us All

Vulnerability doesn't only benefit you—it helps others. By being open and vulnerable with someone else, you let them know several things.

First of all, being vulnerable with someone signals to them that they matter to you. Rather heartbreakingly, a lot of my friends may have spent large chunks of time thinking they didn't really matter to me. Why would they? I was always fine, happy, self-sufficient, and a little bit too busy for them. I was impenetrable. This is terrible on two counts: one, that these glorious people thought I wasn't madly in love with them and needing them in my lives, and two, that they were unable to be there for me in my times of need, because they never saw them.

Secondly, vulnerability tells your loved ones that you trust them. Being offered a piece of someone's darkness, struggle, heartbreak, or even deep joy (because it doesn't always have to be something bad to vulnerable—our joys say just as much about our heart's desires as our sorrows) shows me that I am worthy, and that means a lot. It is an honour that, I think, most people don't take lightly.

Thirdly, being vulnerable and open with someone shows them that you want a deeper relationship with them and that they can share things with you. Most people are innately aware of the balance of reciprocity in their relationships: we want to keep things "even" and give to each other in balance with what we get, whether that involves taking turns buying rounds at the pub or the level of our hearts we divulge. If we give and give and get nothing in return, we start to feel taken advantage of. If we keep receiving and never give back, we feel like moochers. We want to share these deep connections in a balanced kind of way.

Imbalance can be a powerful social cue that two people are not on the same page about something, and if it is an imbalance of vulnerability, then that something is probably investment in the relationship.

Sometimes what's under the surface can feel too deep or ridiculous to share. When I was in my depressive states, I would often think,

"What, am I supposed to just call up a friend and say that I hate myself?" Well, the answer is pretty much yes. Call someone you trust. They can give you perspective, they can talk you through the crappy feelings, and they can help you see the other side. And, if those feelings are too far and too deep for them to handle, maybe they can help you find help elsewhere.

There is one more way vulnerability can help others: it can help them see themselves in you. This creates all sorts of bonding and understanding, as well as that wonderful feeling of "I'm not alone" that we all crave. Since I started trying to turn off my "everything's great" default and let people see the actual vulnerable stuff that's part of me, I have seen more than once a look cross my friends' faces. The look was a mixture of relief, connection, understanding, and compassion. They were surprised. Not only, I gather, because it was new information, but because they thought that I was full of perspective and happiness at all times. There seemed to be an expression of, "If someone else can feel this way about herself, I'm not so crazy to feel this way about myself."

It helped. We connected. We saw something of ourselves in each other and found some solace together. So here I am, perhaps with a touch of hubris that what I have to say might help on a larger scale, hoping you'll see a bit of yourself in me.

I can't guarantee that everyone you open up to will prove to be trustworthy, that none of them will hurt you or disappoint you. They are human beings, too. But I can tell you that, overall, in the long run, it is worth it to take the risk and let people in. This is where it's possible to find the deep, authentic connection we all need.

For a fantastic analysis of vulnerability, I would highly recommend reading anything written by Brené Brown. I would start with *Daring Greatly* as a gentle-yet-tough push into the vital importance of vulnerability. She is a social scientist who has researched shame and vulnerability in depth. Like many great writers, her work doesn't necessarily uncover anything new—the concept of vulnerability is as old as human society—but it unpacks the reality of living an open, heartfelt life in a very real way.

Chapter 15: Living with Purpose

"Don't aim at success. The more you aim at it and make it your target, the more you are going to miss it. For success, like happiness, cannot be pursued; it must ensue, and it only does so as the unintended side effect of one's personal dedication to a cause greater than oneself." - Viktor E. Frankl

"Those who have a 'why' to live, can bear with almost any 'how'." - Viktor E. Frankl

Viktor Frankl was a Jewish psychologist in the 1940s in Austria, and sadly, we all know what that means: he spent many years in a concentration camp.

Frankl survived, and part of what got him through the experience of the concentration camps was counselling other prisoners. He pulled several of them back from the brink of suicide, and the way he did it was to help them determine their purpose in life. Frankl believed that everyone has a unique purpose that only they can fulfill, and that depression (and many other emotional disorders) are often cured by discovering one's purpose.

In the concentration camps, it motivated people to get out alive. One man had a scientific paper he had been working on that he needed to get out and complete. Another had children waiting for him on the other side.

Frankl said it best in his book *Man's Search for Meaning*: "Everyone has his own specific vocation or mission in life; everyone must carry out a concrete assignment that demands fulfillment. Therein he cannot be replaced, nor can his life be repeated, thus, everyone's task is unique as his specific opportunity to implement it."

From a Task to a Mission

I would like to take this a step beyond what Frankl said about fulfillment and concrete assignments. I love his point about having a purpose and being irreplaceable for that purpose. I also love that he describes it as a concrete assignment, and I don't think he's wrong. It can be incredibly useful to determine what your assignment is. But if you make it too concrete, well, what happens when you achieve it? Hopefully, you think of something else and start chipping away at that, but how do you know what that should, or could, be?

Here's where my slight variation on Frankl's theme comes into play. Beyond the question, "What is your purpose," I would challenge you to ask yourself, "What is your mission?"

A mission is not a task, nor is it a vocation. The answer to this question isn't a job or career. It's a calling. It's a broader definition of Frankl's purpose: a driving force that shapes all the choices you make, the kinds of jobs you look for, and the assignments you pursue. It can be anything.

One of my friends sees his mission as being an advocate for the oppressed. Currently, he works making documentaries for mission-based organizations revealing the plights of oppressed groups, which is a perfect way to live out his mission. He could, however, take a different job—he could be a writer, a lawyer, a politician, or any other number of things and work towards this calling.

Another friend sees herself as made to help people understand each other better—specifically people who might be misunderstood for being thought of as different, scary, or an outsider. Currently, she writes plays. She wrote one about a girl with a developmental disorder, one about a guy in a biker gang, and another about a psychopath, all helping audiences broaden their understanding of groups that might be marginalized or othered.

Personally, I think my mission is to help people understand themselves. Part of that mission lives in my writing this book, and I also believe my day job serves that function as well. I work for a theatre company that specializes in putting on plays that explore the spiritual side of life. I am helping bring people into a theatre so that they can see a play that will, I believe, help them understand themselves better. I am a part of the mission. It also makes sense, then, that the other vocation I almost pursued (and still might one day) is that of a counsellor.

So, what's your mission in life? What's your calling? What excites you? What cause makes you feel like your guts are being tied up in knots or pulled out of your body? What cause would you work hard for, even if it means doing tasks you don't particularly care for? Data entry or cleaning floors can become a lot more meaningful when it's part of a job that serves a cause you care about.

I'm not talking about the "follow your bliss, jump out of bed with joy every Monday morning, take your passion and make it happen"-type mantras. While waking up every morning thrilled about every aspect of your job sounds amazing, I don't know that it is particularly realistic. Every job, and every life, no matter how wonderful, has elements that are boring, frustrating, or just plain crappy.

If we only pursue excitement or fun in our work, we are missing the bigger picture. This isn't about finding one thing to do that excites you all the time, but the meaning behind it all. Once you find a meaning that fires you up, not only will you have a clearer picture of work that might bring you more day-to-day joy, but it provides context for the boring drudgery that is bound to come up and makes it worthwhile. Any job can serve a mission.

Finding my mission was another element that helped me in my journey of self-appreciation. Understanding what I could contribute to the world and how I could help make it a better place gave me a sense of meaning to my existence. Not only was I not a waste of space, but I could actually add value to those around me. It was very empowering.

You might not know what your mission is yet, and it may change over the course of your life. One of the most freeing things in my life was to realize that I didn't have to tie myself down to a previously-held dream. My life's work could change into something unforeseen, and that was okay. So whether you have never found your mission, or you feel like it might be morphing into something new, pay attention to that little tickle in the back of your brain. Follow your righteous indignation, deep sorrow, or all-encompassing joy. Powerful reactions usually point to something meaningful. What does your joy celebrate? What does your righteous indignation want to protect? What does your deep sorrow mourn for?

Frederick Buechner is a very smart theologian who has written extensively about the journey of life and finding meaning therein. On the subject of purpose, he suggested going "Where your deep gladness meets the world's deep hunger" in his book *Wishful Thinking*.

Where is a need that you would be glad to fulfill, and how do you feel about yourself knowing you could make a difference?

Chapter 16: With a Childhood

"Children begin by loving their parents; as they grow older they judge them; sometimes they forgive them." - Oscar Wilde

With all the time I have spent in counselling, it may surprise you that my childhood didn't come up until the most recent round. I have always been very resistant to the tendency that exists among some therapists, or at least representations of therapy in the media, in which they ask their clients to examine their childhoods and parental relationships for the roots of the wounds they carry into adulthood. I felt this approach placed blame on childhood events and parents that seemed unnecessary and perhaps even unfair. I didn't think this approach applied to me because I am lucky enough to feel like I have amazing parents, and I felt guilty at the idea of blaming them for my problems. I always knew they loved me, I always loved them, and they treated me well. What's the problem?

The problem, of course, they were human. So, too, were the other people who made up my world as a child: friends, other family, teachers, classmates, neighbours. Overall, I would say they were good and caring people, but some of them did things that made me feel terrible—things that wounded me in ways that remain with me to this day.

What I learned in a most recent round of counselling is that exploring and validating my childhood wounds does not mean I am laying blame on individuals or events. I am simply finding the source of my ongoing wounds, large and small, so that I can work towards letting them heal.

We all have these wounds. They are pains that emerged in childhood when we were rejected, beat up, belittled, assaulted, or told, one way or another, that we had no power or that we were not enough. We developed coping mechanisms to work through these pains because, at the time, that's what we needed to do to survive. These coping mechanisms can take as many forms as there are hurts. They may have consisted of developing a long list of mental tests to see if someone really loved us enough; pre-emptively rejecting others before they could reject us; working vigilantly to be perfect, keeping so busy that we are unattainable; becoming small and unnoticeable; becoming big and attention-grabbing; or never putting any real effort into anything because of the perceived inevitability of failure or a desire to avoid attention that might become dangerous.

These practices made sense at the time. It's what we had to do to get through life as children in a scary, and maybe dangerous, world. Your childhood self could not get through your so-called friends' bullying, your teachers' scorn, your parents' abandonment, or other pains without these tactics.

As life progresses into adulthood, however, the original threat from childhood is likely gone. But the coping behaviours remain. And now there is a cost to their persistence—as they lose their utility, they start to hurt us. As adults, the actions that kept us emotionally and psychologically safe and alive growing up may be keeping us from forming real connections with other people. This could be because we actively push them away as a test of their affection ("if they really love me they will fight for me"), or make it impossible for them to see us ("every time people get close I get hurt, so I will be invisible"), or refuse to take care of ourselves, resulting in hygiene problems ("I am dirty and disgusting on the inside, so what is even the point in pretending otherwise?"). This may seem impossible, especially if you don't yet value yourself enough to see why another person might want to connect with you. Sometimes we can fake it until we make it, acting as if we are loveable by shedding some armour and giving ourselves the chance to experience acceptance. Other times, especially with deeper wounds, we will need to spend some time nourishing ourselves and find a sense of worth first. We need to find a way to let those childhood coping behaviours go and step, with terror and bravery, into the world without the armour we've developed.

I've already mentioned my ongoing insecurities about feeling left out. I grew up feeling like I was often on the outside of my relationships—like there was an inner circle my friends and family were all a part of and I was just adjacent to it. I felt like I never fully fit in and I was never fully wanted. It was very lonely, and so one of my coping mechanisms was to be so busy and have so many different groups of friends that it wouldn't matter that I was left out because there was always something to do or someone else to talk to. The cost of this is that I wound up just where I feared I would be: consistently left out of things because I never had time to become truly embedded in a group of friends.

Today, managing and reducing the hectic schedule is a work in progress. But with help, I was able to look back on my past wounds and the initial events in my life that made me feel excluded. While looking back and recognizing them didn't change anything that happened, it helped me to see that past for what it was and take steps to be free of it now.

I think it's most helpful to do this kind of thing with the guidance of a counsellor or therapist. Personal reflection on all this is great, but a counsellor knows what kind of questions to ask to get you to the core of the matter, all while being able to safely bring you back if things get too intense.

As a person who has done a lot of self-analysis, I would have thought I could work through my childhood wounds on my own. I was aware of what they were and that they were likely affecting me now, but the truth is that I could only get so far without an outside ear and voice to help me process it. My counsellor provided an external perspective on my own experience as well as the broader situations, compassion for my pain, and the ability to see patterns I had not recognized. She helped me see simple ways that these wounds were impacting me now, as well as some tools to work through them now, as an adult, with renewed perspective and fresh eyes.

Chapter 17: How to Be a Grown-up

"I don't think I'd have been in such a hurry to reach adulthood if I'd known the whole thing was going to be ad-libbed." - Bill Watterson

Sometimes I wonder if I'm ever going to feel like a grown-up. Every major adult milestone I reach, like moving out, graduating university, or getting my first "real" job seems to arrive at the right time for me. Yet through it all, a part of me feels I've somehow fooled the world into thinking I'm not a hyperactive 13-year-old who's high on Pixie Stix.

Still, from the moment I moved into a dorm for university when I was 18, I felt the glow of independent life as a grown-up. Going grocery shopping, doing laundry, being the only person who decides when I do things, where I go, and what state my room is was (and still is) truly awesome. Yet many of these grown-up tasks still befuddle me, and I'll suddenly realize that a month has gone by and I haven't talked to my parents (who I love talking to and want to stay connected with) or that two months have gone by and I haven't done any laundry (because I own a lot of underwear to get away with that). Plus, why did no one warn me how much of my adult life would be spent washing dishes or how complicated it can be to manage things like health insurance?

The charm of being a bumbling, not-quite-keeping-up-with-life scatterbrain wears off quite quickly. Personally, I feel much better about myself if I'm approaching life with more intention. It feels good to feel grown-up (as long as the heart stays young, but I don't foresee any trouble there). Being able to competently and independently take care of myself became an important part of connecting, reviving, and nourishing my sense of self-worth. There is something very affirming about knowing that I am on top of things, that my life is somewhat organized, that I'll have access to the things I need when I need them, and that people can count on me.

This can be part of an "outside-in" method of self-care. Sometimes it helps to pretend that we are more capable than we feel like we are. Here are some of the ways I set myself up for success when it comes to keeping life on track.

Use Your Technology

Oh my word, smartphones are the best thing ever. Sure, my eyesight and attention span immediately dropped when I got my smartphone, but it's worth it.

First, the calendar: I resisted digitizing my calendar for a long time, but being able to easily edit, track, and share my various appointments is incredible.

Even better, however, are the reminders. I have a biweekly reminder to change my sheets (seriously), as well as daily reminders to take medication and check my calendar. If I ever need to remember something at a specific time and it's not an event to go in the calendar, it gets a reminder, even if it's a task that doesn't seem that important. Why waste mental energy trying to remember a thing? If you want to remember to make a reservation at 5pm when the restaurant opens, set a reminder and set your mind at ease. I used to rely heavily on lists in notebooks, but you have to remember to look at your list for it to be useful. Reminders pop up on your phone and computer and, as long as you don't ignore them, guarantee that the right idea will invade your brain at the right moment.

Always Be Prepared

I want to eat vegetables all the time, because they will help my body function as I stay alive longer, but I also don't really love the prep work involved in cooking. And by "don't really love" I mean "can't stand." I have found that the only way I will eat my vegetables is if, as soon as I buy them, I chop them up into whatever configuration makes them easiest to snack on or cook with and put them in a big Tupperware container.

Maybe the veggie thing doesn't matter to you, but what else can you prepare in advance so you actually do the things you want to do? In the world of life coaching, this is referred to as "removing barriers", a practice that involves anticipating the things that make it harder for you to accomplish tasks or goals and pre-emptively managing them. Pre-chopping my veggies removes the barrier of having to deal with them later when I'm hungry and impatient.

If you want to exercise in the mornings, get your workout gear all ready to go the night before so you have one less excuse to get out of it when you wake up. If you want to track your spending, use cash or download a banking app. If you want to make more green smoothies, keep your blender on the counter instead of stashing it away in a cupboard and prep your ingredients in advance. Removing barriers is putting the work into something in advance, so that later when you are faced with the challenge of following through on your goals, it's as easy as possible.

It can seem like a rigid way to live life, but really it's more like streamlining. You need to structure your life to make space for the things you want to do. Besides, I feel much better about myself when I actually do these things that I want to do than if I have such an unstructured, freewheeling life that they never happen.

Clean as You Go

I have finally come to terms with the fact that my mom was right: having a clean and tidy home does feel good. First of all, it helps me feel better in that I'm no longer embarrassed when people come over. Secondly, with a tidy home, I can walk around without feeling like it's closing in on me or like I must remain constantly vigilant to avoid stepping on things. However, I am a busy lady and things easily pile up.

These days, as much as I can, I clean as I go, especially with dishes. I find I'm very unlikely to get off the couch or stop doing something fun because it's time to clean, but I don't really mind tacking a little extra time on cleaning while I'm already up and moving around. So washing the dishes while I'm cooking is way better than cleaning up after a meal. A friend of mine likes to "race the kettle:" when she puts the kettle on for a cup of tea, she tries to get as much tidying done as she can while she waits. I love this concept because it makes cleaning up fast, and a little sense of competition can be motivating, even if it's against no one but yourself. These little bite-size cleaning sessions don't take care of everything of course, but it makes the job more manageable when it's time to force myself to get to work.

Go to Bed

Going to bed at a reasonable hour and waking up at a reasonable hour just feels good. How you define "reasonable" is up to you. I used to feel like going to bed between 12am and 1am, then waking up between 8am and 9am, was the key to feeling good and productive. Now, I'd rather go to bed around 10pm and wake up around 6am. I learned over the years that mornings were the only time I could claim purely as my own, and that time became precious. Before work, I can set the tone for my day, write, do yoga, eat breakfast, and simply do some things for myself before my schedule becomes overrun with the demands of work, friends, and family. I am able to actually tune into myself and feel like my life doesn't just exist for other people.

Going to bed in time to get a good night's sleep can be really hard, especially if you have insomnia or sleep issues related to depression or anxiety. For serious insomnia issues, I highly recommend speaking to a counsellor, doctor, or other health professional. You may benefit from a variety of sleep therapy techniques.

If it's more a matter of will and planning, as it was for me, then I found great success by setting an alarm on my phone to snap me out of whatever I was doing and remind me that it was time for bed. I also start getting ready for bed much earlier than seems necessary so that there is time to move slowly, get interrupted, and still get some reading in before bed. Building a routine around your bedtime can serve as a wonderful signal to your brain and body that it's time for bed. Whether it's taking a quick shower, rubbing lotion into your feet, taking a moment to write in a journal, or doing some simple stretches, give yourself the space to take care of yourself before bed. And of course, we could all do with less screen time, especially before bed. Be generous with your time the first time you try to do this—you don't have to start a full hour before your ideal bedtime, but give yourself space to enjoy the process, unwind, and take care of yourself.

Going to bed at an hour that allows you to wake up and feel good about your day, whatever time that is, is an important part of honouring yourself. Reflect on when you feel the most alive and when you want to get things done and take care of yourself by building in some practices to help make that happen.

Use Passwords for Good

You can use your passwords to remind you of the things you really want in life. We have to type in passwords about a million times a day, so why not use them to remind us of something we want?

I read an article about a man who had just gone through a divorce. He made his password "forgive@her," and then every time he checked his email, his computer went to sleep, or he otherwise had to type a password in, he was reminded of his desire to forgive his ex-wife.

You can use a password as a personal reminder for anything you'd like to strengthen your intentions for in your life, such as reminding yourself to be grateful, of a goal you have, to do your dishes, to save your money. So much in my experience of wellness has come from little built-in reminders and practices of my intentions and goals, from gratitude journals to stolen moments of meditation.

The common practice of typing in a password is the perfect time to insert a little bit of intention.

The older I get, the more I realize that anyone seeming to "have it all together" is an illusion. The people who seem to always be on top of everything are not superior beings who keep track of everything in their heads and have perfect self-control. They have systems, routines, and reminders that keep them on track. This realization relieved a lot of the pressure I was putting on myself to meet this imagined standard for existence, and also set me free to create the necessary circumstances for me to live my life in a way that makes me feel sane and competent. This has been a huge value to my feelings of contribution to the world and sense of self-worth.

Conclusion

That's it. That is my experience of the daily practices, trials, and work it took for me to begin living a life where self-loathing and hopelessness are not the status quo. It's my movement in the ongoing journey towards feeling better about myself and my life.

I will be honest, my brain is still not always my friend. It has had a lot of practice going to some pretty dark places, so it can go there quickly and easily, assuming that I am friendless or otherwise alone, that I don't have anything to offer, and that I am best left forgotten. Now, however, those dark thoughts and feelings don't have nearly the same hold they used to. My head and my heart both know, in a very deep place, that I have value, that I am loved and loveable, and that I have something to offer the world. I actually like the person who I am – if I met her out in the world, I might even want to be friends with her. I still have to deal with depression from time to time, but now my baseline is different. I am starting from the foundation of actually believing in my intrinsic value and that I am worth something. This is huge. Battling depression from a place of knowing my intrinsic worth completely changed the game for me.

One of the biggest, and best, changes, though is that I am no longer trying to live through everything alone. I have friends who I am vulnerable and open with as well as a counsellor who I see when it feels like I need help. One of the worst things that our anxiety, depression, and self-loathing do is isolate us in our misery. It is a huge relief not having to do everything on my own.

If I could leave you with one thought, it would be to take your wins where they come, no matter how small. Pay attention to the little seed of hope within you that pushed you to seek a better way of living by reading this book. Every moment of awareness, every positive practice, every instance of shared gratitude, tallies up and strengthens your ability to keep going and find your true worth. You might feel changes in quick bursts or barely-perceptible slowness, but it's worth it to continue. You deserve to live life free from the weight of self-loathing.

I really hope that my experiences shed some light on your own and that something in here was helpful for your own journey. Almost everything I have included here is an adaptation and amalgamation of experiences from multiple sources, and I encourage you to continue the tradition by altering my practices as needed to fit into your life.

Please feel free to be in touch if you have any questions or want to share an experience of your own. I'd love to hear from you! You can find me at andrealoewen.com[1].

---

1. http://www.andrealoewen.com/

References and Recommended Readings

Chapter 1

"You love a person because he or she has lovable traits, but you accept everyone just because they're alive and human." - *In His Own Words* by Albert Ellis

"The purpose of life is not to be happy. It is to be useful, to be honorable, to be compassionate, to have it make some difference that you have lived and lived well." - Leo C. Rosten in his essay "The Myths by Which We Live" (often misattributed to Ralph Waldo Emerson)

The Humans by Matt Haig

Chapter 3

The Molecules of Emotion by Candace Pert

The Empirical Status of Cognitive-Behavioural Therapy: A review of meta-analyses: http://www.sciencedirect.com/science/article/pii/S0272735805001005

Chapter 5

Attitude of Gratitude by M.J. Ryan

Chapter 6

Radical Gratitude by Mary Jo Leddy

Chapter 7

How to Put More Time Into Your Life by Dru Scott

Julie and Julia: My Year of Cooking Dangerously by Julie Powell.

Chapter 9

Quirkyalone by Sasha Cagen

Chapter 10

Why Marriages Succeed or Fail by Dr. John Gottman

The Five Love Languages by Dr. Gary Chapman

How to Make Someone Fall in Love With You in 90 Minutes by Nicholas Boothman

Chapter 11

Perfect Love, Imperfect Relationships by John Welwood

Chapter 12

Making Habits, Breaking Habits by Jeremy Dean

Chapter 14

Daring Greatly by Brene Brown

Chapter 15

A Man's Search for Meaning by Viktor Frankl

Wishful Thinking by Frederick Buechner

Acknowledgements

You know, I never read the acknowledgements in other authors' books, because they're just a list of names of people I don't know. Now I am overwhelmed with gratitude for so many people that I wish I could force everyone to read this whole section, hug the page to their chest, and whisper, "thank you" to each person listed here. Did you know that writing a book is a group activity?

Jackie Wong, my editor. I am insanely lucky that Andrea sent me your way! (This is another Andrea, by the way, we're taking over the world.) Your feedback and insights were more than I ever could have dreamed of, and you held my little book, and heart, with such care while you shaped it into something so much better than I could have made on my own. THANK YOU THANK YOU THANK YOU! The more I work with editors, the more I realize that they deserve top billing everywhere. (And Andrea Warner, for introducing me to Jackie!)

Sabrina Miso and Manuela Camisasca for your incredible work getting this book designed and promoted. You are amazing!

Beta readers Paige Louter, Diana Squires, Kaitlin Williams, and Dr. Ruth Wiebe. Early editor Keri Haywood.

My parents and family for being the reason I exist and became a person who likes to make things and occasionally finish them.

Theatre, for teaching me how to dream a big project and then make it happen and know that if it fails it's not the end of the world. (Or at least how to tell myself that.)

Others for support and inspiration: Meaghan Brister, Alison Chisholm, Jennifer Pielak, Zoe Grams, and Lucia Frangione.

My cat, Miss Gertie Marie, for warming my lap while I worked on this beast.

Essex Edwards. You are so supportive, it's ridiculous. I love you!

CPSIA information can be obtained
at www.ICGtesting.com
Printed in the USA
BVHW040536110720
583496BV00005B/19

9 781999 506407